THE HOLY SACRIFICE OF THE MASS

Ladder of Sanctity

THE HOLY SACRIFICE OF THE MASS

Ladder of Sanctity

by
Dom Eugène Vandeur, OSB

Translated from the French by
Clara Morris Rumball, MA

This authorized English translation was made from the French original *La Sainte Messe: Échelle de a Saintetè par Dom Eugène Vandeur, Moine Bénédictin,* 1930 edition, published by Gabriel Beauchesne, Paris, and containing the *Imprimi Potest* by the Right Rev. Abbot Célestin Golenvaux of the Abbey of Maredsous and *Imprimatur* by the Most Rev. Justin Cawet, Coadjutor Bishop of Namur.

This revised edition, © 2023 by The Cenacle Press at Silverstream Priory, incorporates some minor corrections to the text.

Nihil Obstat
Jacobus H. Griffiths, STD
Censor Librorum

Imprimatur
Thomas Edmundus Molloy, STD
Episcopus Brooklyniensis

Brooklynii
xxviii Septembris 1936

All reservable rights reserved.

The Cenacle Press at Silverstream Priory
Silverstream Priory
Stamullen, County Meath, K32 T189, Ireland
www.cenaclepress.com

ISBN 978-1-915544-80-3

Interior layout by Kenneth Lieblich
Cover design by Silverstream Priory

TO
JESUS CHRIST
TRUE GOD AND TRUE MAN
PRIEST, HOST, ALTAR
OF HIS SACRIFICE
EXAMPLE, LAW, HOPE
OF THE SAINTS,
THIS ENTIRE PROFESSION
OF FAITH AND LOVE
AT THE HOLY ALTAR.
AMEN.

INTRODUCTION

Lay participation in the public prayer of the Church has become in our times closer and more widespread. Two decades ago, it was a rare sight to behold the man or woman in the pews reading out of a Missal the self-same prayers uttered by the priest at the altar. But now, those who have sufficient learning, or indeed, many with no learning but with intelligence, have substituted the Missal for the non-liturgical prayerbook, have ceased to murmur the Rosary prayers, and have silently linked their words and their thoughts with the voice of the Church. The faithful have learned the Mass, through lectures and illustration, through Sunday leaflets and explanatory pamphlets. They now understand that they are one with the priest as he offers the Holy Sacrifice, truly though in a lesser degree than the offering priest is one with the High Priest, Jesus. Coincident with this growing and deeper appreciation of oneness between priest and people is the increase in knowledge of the doctrine of the Mystical Body whereby all of us are not only attached to and participators in Christ Jesus but are a part of Him.

Since the contemporary liturgical movement has so well initiated the faithful into the understanding of the Mass, a volume of this type is needed to carry the faithful further into the ascetical and mystical meanings of the Sacrifice. Other books and other instructions have treated, for the laity, the scientific construction, the origin and the historical development, the rubrics and the significance of the Mass, and the laity well comprehend the cold and scholarly facts. There is no reason why the unordained man or woman should not seek, should not absorb, should not be filled with the higher devotional virtues, should not partake of the spiritual ecstasy inherent in the Holy Sacrifice. Accepting the figure of Dom Eugène Vandeur, not only priestly feet are invited to climb the Ladder of Sanctity, but the feet of every man and woman may find place thereon and may ascend. No one is excluded from the elevated altitudes of holiness. No one is refrained from nestling his head, as did John, upon the shoulder of the Saviour. The holy thoughts that a priest has as he ascends to the altar of oblation, those same thoughts and aspirations may be in the souls of those who humbly kneel, motionless, removed from the altar steps.

 These meditations, it is true, were written primarily for priests. The thoughts these pages express, the aspirations they suggest, the offerings they prompt to make, the prayers they formulate, the union with Jesus they produce are for the souls of those marked with the indelible seal. But not only for those but for all who in the wider sense, like Our Lady, like the lay Saints, belong to the Royal Priesthood. It is important, it is necessary that the laity in these troubled times be urged to enter further into the more intelligent devotional sanctity too often regarded as the reservation of the priest and the Religious. My insistence that this book for priests is also a meditation book for the laity is prompted by the example of the lady who has translated it. She read it in French, and prayed it while she attended Mass. Only after she had experienced in her own soul the unction of it, she a married woman, did she set herself the work of turning it into English for other married and single men and women as well as for the priest.

 But it is the priest who will benefit the most from these short meditations. How many of us lose the feeling of the great spiritual adventure as we grow older. How many of us grow habituated to the daily recital of the prayers of the Mass, so that, knowing them by heart, we are not struck daily by their meanings and are not lifted up daily by their unction. We recall, as the author reminds us frequently, the awe that filled us in our Masses when we were young priests, the ecstasy and exaltation that thrilled through us as we pronounced each word from the *Introibo* to the *Veritatis*. We have thought deeply, we have prayed fervently, we have tried to encompass the majesty of the daily Sacrifice in which "that same Christ is contained and immolated in an unbloody manner who once offered Himself in a bloody manner on the altar of the Cross." (Session XXII, Council of Trent). But we need continually to remind ourselves, sanctified and anointed in the Lord as we are, through meditations such as these, that we must ever be climbing the Ladder of Sanctity, through Contrition of the Soul, as in the first part of the Mass, through Illumination of the Spirit, as in the Introit, through Union of the Will, as from the Offertory to the end. A day-by-day meditation on the words of the Mass will be of inestimable help in the day-by-day celebration of the Mass. The good priest, the striving priest, the priest longing for his God will be invigorated through these meditations with a newer spiritual uplift, and will celebrate with deeper love for his Lord what the ancient Christians termed the Mystery of the Great Action.

Francis X. Talbot, SJ

TRANSLATOR'S PREFACE

Conscious though she must be of the impossibility of doing justice to the original French of Dom Vandeur's contemplative work, the translator feels none the less a great satisfaction, which proceeds almost equally from her sense of gratitude for the privilege of handling so intimately a work which has been most instructive and helpful to her personally, as from her happiness in making it available to others, not only to the great priesthood of "the order of Melchisedech," but to common Catholics like herself.

Her sense of inadequacy would be endlessly greater, however, were it not for the generous aid she has continually received in her labor. She desires, therefore, to acknowledge herewith her debt of gratitude to all the following: the Reverend John F. Donovan, of Our Lady of Angels Parish, Brooklyn, to whose inspiration, encouragement, and active interest the success of the work is in large measure due; Sister M. Rosaria, PH.D, Sister Superior of Our Lady of Angels Convent, Brooklyn, for her criticism, and her supervision of the preparation, of the MS; the Rev. James H. Griffiths, STD, Vice-Chancellor of the Diocese of Brooklyn, to whom the translator has had constant recourse for final critical judgment and information and whose command of French and Theology has made doubly valuable his critical reading and checking of the MS; the Rev. Mansour Stephen, Pastor of the Maronite Church of Our Lady of Lebanon, Brooklyn, who has given much practical aid; and the Rev. Francis X. Talbot, SJ, Editor of *America*, through whose kind interest Dom Vandeur's work will be given to American readers. Also, since it must ever be an inestimable boon to the harassed translator to see how another has wrestled with a foreign idiom, she takes this opportunity to express her appreciation of the beautiful German translation of the Rev. Ignatius Rollenmüller, OSB,[1] kindly brought to her attention by the Rev. George S. Herget.

---

1 *Das heilige Meßopfer, Führer zur Heiligkeit*, Regensburg: Friedrich Pustet, 1933.

AUTHOR'S PREFACE

Urged by frequent requests, we undertook the revision, indeed, the total recasting of our *Notes sur la liturgie de la Messe*,[1] the last edition of which had long since been exhausted. Everything was carefully set forth and made clear. For twenty-five years this Holy Mass had been the subject of our study and our preaching. And what could be more worthy of the apostolic zeal of the priest of Jesus Christ? Every time the Holy Mass is celebrated, is not the work of Redemption accomplished? Is it not the constant source, through the Holy Mysteries it commemorates and renews, of all sanctity? *Sacrosancta mysteria, in quibus omnis sanctitatis fontem constituisti.*[2] By teaching a soul what the Holy Mass is and how to live by it, do we not at the same time renew our hold on this soul, if necessary, converting it, giving it up to repentance, causing it to be penetrated with the light of Faith, melted in the fire of love? In a word, do we not thereby lead it to sanctity?

Now, in order to obtain this result, it is not sufficient simply to explain scientifically what the Mass is; nor can it suffice to give its component parts and the history of its rites and ceremonies. That is all useful; in truth it is most necessary! And nevertheless we need something more, something better: we must make clear its ascetic and mystical significance by initiating souls into the interior life nourished by this Gift of God which is the Holy Mass.

This is the sole aim of our Meditations. Taking in review the *Ordinary* of the Mass, they attempt to trace therein significant stages of intense spiritual life which, through the practice of sacrifice and more and more complete renunciation, will elevate the soul to perfect union with God. From this viewpoint we find the Holy Mass has the appearance of a sublime Ladder of Sanctity.

The *Ordinary* itself contains the highly doctrinal *Proper* of the Mass of *Corpus Christi*. The teachings set forth in this Mass have so much to say

---

1 *La Sainte Messe, Notes sur sa Liturgie*, 8th edition, 1928.
2 These most holy mysteries in which Thou hast set the fount of all holiness (Secret of the Mass of St Ignatius Loyola).

concerning this sanctity that they may serve as a complement to the ascetic and mystical study of the Ordinary.

We venture to hope that our work will find acceptance among the priests of Jesus Christ, who by their vocation—at once so formidable and so lovingly gratuitous—are obliged to live from the Mass in order to become saints.

In our opinion it will be very useful to all the faithful, eager also to receive in their own souls the flood of sanctifying and redemptive graces that flows from the altar.

By intention, these meditations are brief; they permit the reader to linger at will over the ideas presented. By the inspiration of the Holy Spirit, these thoughts will give birth to others which will be better surely and at any rate helpful.

Our whole purpose is to lead each one who meditates or contemplates to make his own life a perfect holocaust, the sacred oblation of which will be as it were another eucharist or thanksgiving proclaiming and glorifying the divine Eucharist, in which Jesus Christ has made Himself Priest, Host, and very Altar of His Sacrifice. The whole Christian life consists in this renunciation of self in union with the self-renunciation of the Saviour of men, the only One *through Whom, with Whom, and in Whom all honor and glory is to God the Father almighty in the unity of the Holy Ghost for ever and ever. Amen.*

Dom Eugène Vandeur, OSB

Monastery of St Benedict of Maredsous
Feast of *Corpus Christi*
MCMXXIX

DOCTRINE ON
THE SACRIFICE OF THE MASS[1]

The Holy Council of Trent teaches as follows: "forasmuch as, under the former Testament, according to the testimony of the Apostle Paul, there was no perfection, because of the weakness of the Levitical priesthood (Heb. 7: 11–18); there was need, God, the Father of mercies, so ordaining, that another priest should rise, according to the order of Melchisedech (v. 11), our Lord Jesus Christ, Who might consummate, and lead to what is perfect, as many as were to be sanctified. He, therefore, our God and Lord, though He was about to offer Himself once on the altar of the Cross unto God the Father, by means of His death (Heb. 9: 5), there to operate an eternal redemption (v. 12); nevertheless, because that His priesthood was not to be extinguished by His death, in the last supper, on the night in which He was betrayed—that He might leave, to His own beloved Spouse the Church, a visible sacrifice, such as the nature of man requires, whereby that bloody sacrifice, once to be accomplished on the Cross, might be represented, and the memory thereof remain even unto the end of the world, and its salutary virtue be applied to the remission of those sins which we daily commit—declaring Himself constituted a priest for ever, according to the order of Melchisedech (Ps. 109: 4). He offered up to God the Father His own Body and Blood under the species of bread and wine; and, under the symbols of these same things, He delivered (His own Body and Blood) to be received by His Apostles, whom He then constituted priests of the New Testament; and by those words, Do this in commemoration of me (Luke 22: 19), He commanded them and their successors in the priesthood, to offer (them); even as the Catholic Church has always understood and taught. For, having celebrated the ancient Passover, which the multitude of the children of Israel immolated in memory of their going out of Egypt, He instituted the new Passover (to wit): Himself to be immolated, under

---

[1] Session XXII from *The Canons and Decrees of the Council of Trent*, translated by the Rev. J. Waterworth.

visible signs, by the Church through (the ministry of) priests, in memory of His own passage from this world unto the Father, when by the effusion of His own Blood He redeemed us, and delivered us from the power of darkness, and translated us into His kingdom. And this is indeed that clean oblation, which cannot be defiled by any unworthiness, or malice of those that offer (it); which the Lord foretold by Melachias was to be offered in every place, clean to His name, which was to be great amongst the Gentiles (Mal. 1: 11); and which the Apostle Paul, writing to the Corinthians, has not obscurely indicated, when he says that they who are defiled by the participation of the table of devils cannot be partakers of the table of the Lord (1 Cor. 10: 21); by the table, meaning in both places the altar. This, in fine, is that oblation which was prefigured by various types of sacrifices, during the period of nature, and of the law; in as much as it comprises all the good things signified by those sacrifices, as being the consummation and perfection of them all.

"And forasmuch, as, in this divine sacrifice which is celebrated in the Mass, that same Christ is contained and immolated in an unbloody manner, Who once offered Himself in a bloody manner on the altar of the Cross; the holy Synod teaches that this sacrifice is truly propitiatory and that by means thereof this is effected, that we obtain mercy, and find grace in seasonable aid (Heb. 4: 6), if we draw nigh unto God, contrite and penitent, with a sincere heart and upright faith, with fear and reverence. For the Lord, appeased by the oblation thereof, and granting the grace and gift of penitence, forgives even heinous crimes and sins. For the victim is one and the same, the same now offering by the ministry of priests, Who then offered Himself on the Cross, the manner alone of offering being different. The fruits indeed of which oblation, of that bloody one to wit, are received most plentifully through this unbloody one; so far is this (latter) from derogating in any way from that (former oblation). Therefore, not only for the sins, punishments (*poenis*, pains), satisfactions, and other necessities of the faithful who are living, but also for those who are departed in Christ, and who are not as yet fully purified (*purgatis*, purged), is it rightly offered, agreeably to a tradition of the Apostles.

"And although the Church has been accustomed at times to celebrate certain Masses in honor and memory of the saints; not therefore, however, doth she teach that sacrifice is offered unto them, but unto God alone,

Who crowned them; whence neither is the priest wont to say, 'I offer sacrifice to thee, Peter, or Paul' (St Augustine, *De Civ. Dei*, Lib. viii., c. 27); but, giving thanks to God for their victories, he implores their patronage, that they may vouchsafe to intercede for us in Heaven, whose memory we celebrate upon earth.

"And whereas it beseemeth that holy things be administered in a holy manner, and of all holy things this sacrifice is the most holy; to the end that it might be worthily and reverently offered and received, the Catholic Church instituted, many years ago, the sacred Canon, so pure from every error, that nothing is contained therein which does not in the highest degree savor of a certain holiness and piety, and raise up unto God the minds of those that offer. For it is composed, out of the very words of the Lord, the traditions of the Apostles, and the pious institutions also of holy pontiffs.

"And whereas such is the nature of man, that, without external helps, he cannot easily be raised to the meditation of divine things; therefore has holy Mother Church instituted certain rites, to wit that certain things be pronounced in the Mass in a low, and others in a louder, tone. She has likewise employed ceremonies, such as mystic benedictions, lights, incense, vestments, and many other things of this kind, derived from an apostolical discipline and tradition, whereby both the majesty of so great a sacrifice might be recommended, and the minds of the faithful be excited, by those visible signs of religion and piety, to the contemplation of those most sublime things which are hidden in this sacrifice.

"The sacred and holy Synod would fain indeed that, at each Mass, the faithful who are present should communicate, not only in spiritual desire, but also by the sacramental participation of the Eucharist, that thereby a more abundant fruit might be derived to them from this most holy sacrifice: but not therefore, if this be not always done, does it condemn, as private and unlawful, but approves of and therefore commends, those Masses in which the priest alone communicates sacramentally; since those Masses also ought to be considered as truly common; partly because the people communicate spiritually thereat; partly also because they are celebrated by a public minister of the Church, not for himself only, but for all the faithful, who belong to the Body of Christ.

"The holy Synod notices, in the next place, that it has been enjoined by the Church on priests, to mix water with the wine that is to be offered in the chalice (Synod. Quini-Sext., cap. 32; Conc. Carthag., iii, c. 24; Concil. Flor.); as well because it is believed that Christ the Lord did this, as also because from His side there came out blood and water (John 19: 34); the memory of which mystery is renewed by this commixture; and, whereas in the Apocalypse of blessed John, the peoples are called waters (Apoc. 17: 15), the union of that faithful people with Christ their Head is hereby represented.

"Although the Mass contains great instruction for the faithful people, nevertheless, it has not seemed expedient to the Fathers, that it should be everywhere (*passim,* indiscriminately) celebrated in the vulgar tongue. Wherefore, the ancient usage of each church, and the rite approved of by the holy Roman Church, the mother and mistress of all churches, being in each place retained; and, that the sheep of Christ may not suffer hunger, nor the little ones ask for bread, and there be none to break it unto them (Lam. 4: 4), the holy Synod charges pastors, and all who have the cure of souls, that they frequently, during the celebration of Mass, expound either by themselves, or others, some portion of those things which are read at Mass, and that, amongst the rest, they explain some mystery of this most holy sacrifice, especially on the Lord's Days and festivals."

Most truly, therefore, did St Vincent Ferrer say: "The Mass is the highest act of contemplation that is possible: *Missa est altius opus contemplationis, quod possit esse.*"

CONTENTS

Introduction by Rev. Francis X. Talbot, SJ	vii
Translator's Preface	xi
Author's Preface	xiii
Doctrine on the Sacrifice of the Mass	xv

Contrition of the Soul
Quia Peccavi Nimis

1	In Nomine Patris et Filii et Spiritus Sancti. Amen. *In the Name of the Father, and of the Son, and of the Holy Ghost. Amen.*	5
2	Introibo ad Altare Dei *I will go in unto the Altar of God*	9
3	Judica Me, Deus, Fortitudo Mea *Judge Me, O God, Thou, My Strength*	11
4	Emitte Lucem et Veritatem Tuam *Send Forth Thy Light and Thy Truth*	13
5	In Montem Sanctum et in Tabernacula Tua *Unto Thy Holy Hill and into Thy Tabernacles*	15
6	Confiteor Tibi in Cithara *I will Praise Thee upon the Harp*	17
7	Gloria Patri et Filio et Spiriui Sancto *Glory be to the Father and to the Son and the Holy Ghost*	19
8	Adjutorium Nostrum in Nomine Domini *Our Help is in the Name of the Lord*	21
9	Confiteor Quia Peccavi *I Confess that I have Sinned*	23
10	Deus, Tu Conversus Vivificabis Nos *Thou Shalt Turn Again, O God, and Quicken Us*	25

11	Dominus Vobiscum	
	The Lord Be with You	27
12	Oremus	
	Let Us Pray	29
13	Ad Sancta Sanctorum	
	Into the Holy of Holies	21

Illumination of the Spirit
Credo

14	Cibavit Eos	
	He Fed Them	35
15	Kyrie Eleison	
	Lord, Have Mercy	37
16	Gloria Deo, Pax Hominibus	
	Glory be to God, Peace to Men	39
17	Suscipe Deprecationem	
	Receive Our Prayer	41
18	Deus, Qui Nobis	
	O God, Who to Us	43
19	Sub Sacramento Mirabili	
	In a Wonderful Sacrament	47
20	Passionis Tuae Memoriam	
	A Memorial of Thy Passion	51
21	Redemptionis Tuae Fructum	
	The Fruit of Thy Redemption	53
22	Per Dominum Jesum Christum	
	Through Jesus Christ Our Lord	57
23	Donec Veniat	
	Until He Come	63
24	Probet Seipsum Homo	
	Let a Man Prove Himself	67
25	Animosa Firmat Fides	
	Dauntless Faith Attests	69

26	Caro Mea, Cibus, Sanguis Meus, Potus	
	My Flesh Is Meat Indeed, and My Blood Is Drink Indeed	71
27	In Me Manet et Ego in Illo	
	He Abideth in Me, and I in Him	75
28	Vivet Propter Me	
	He Shall Live by Me	77
29	Credo	
	I Believe	79

Union of the Will
Suscipe

30	Sancti Erunt Deo Suo	
	They Shall Be Holy to Their God	87
31	Ad Gloriam Nominis Sui	
	To the Glory of His Name	91
32	Per Hujus Aquae et Vini Mysterium	
	By the Mystery of This Water and Wine	95
33	Oratio Mea Sicut Incensum	
	Let My Prayer Be Directed as Incense	97
34	Lavabo Inter Innocentes Manus	
	I Will Wash My Hands among the Innocent	99
35	Unitatis et Pacis Dona	
	The Gifts of Unity and Peace	101
36	Sursum Corda	
	Life up Your Hearts	105
37	Gratias Agamus	
	Let Us Give Thanks	107
38	Sanctus, Sanctus, Sanctus	
	Holy, Holy Holy Is the Lord	109
39	Pro Ecclesia Tua	
	For Thy Church	111
40	Memento, Domine	
	Be Mindful, O Lord	113

41	Communicantes	
	Communicating	115
42	Ut Placatus Accipias	
	That Thou Receive Graciously	117
43	Accepit Panem	
	He Took into His Hands the Bread and the Precious Chalice	119
44	Deditque Discipulis; Accipite	
	And Gave to His Disciples, Saying: Take	123
45	Hoc Est Enim Corpus Meum	
	This Is My Body	127
46	Hic Est Enim Calix Sanguinis Mei	
	This Is the Chalice of My Blood	129
47	Haec Facietis	
	Ye Shall Do These Things	131
48	Unde et Memores	
	Wherefore, Calling to Mind	133
49	Digneris et Accepta Habere	
	Do Thou Vouchsafe to Accept	135
50	Jube Haec Perferri	
	Command That These Things Be Borne	137
51	In Christo Quiescentibus	
	To All That Rest in Christ	141
52	Nobis Quoque Peccatoribus	
	To Us Sinners Also	143
53	Per Quem Haec Omnia Bona Creas	
	Through Whom Thou Createst All These Gifts	145
54	Omnis Honor et Gloria	
	All Honor and Glory	147
55	Pater Noster	
	Our Father	151
56	Sanctificetur Nomen Tuum	
	Hallowed Be Thy Name	153
57	Adveniat Regnum Tuum	
	Thy Kingdom Come	155

58	Fiat Voluntas Tua	
	Thy Will Be Done	157
59	Panem Nostrum Quotidianum da Nobis	
	Give Us Our Daily Bread	159
60	Et Dimitte Nobis Sicut et Nos	
	And Forgive Us As We Forgive	161
61	Et Ne Nos Inducas in Tentationem	
	And Lead Us not into Temptation	163
62	Sed Libera Nos a Malo	
	But Deliver Us from Evil	165
63	Pax Domini Sit Semper Vobiscus	
	The Peace of the Lord Be Always with You	167
64	Agnus Dei, Dona Nobis Pacem	
	Lamb of God ... Grant Us Peace	169
65	Pacem Meam do Vobis	
	My Peace I Give unto You	171
66	Me a Te Nunquam Separari Permittas	
	Never Suffer Me to Be Separated from Thee	173
67	Domine, Non Sum Dignus	
	Lord, I am not Worthy	175
68	Corpus ... Sanguis ... Christi Custodiat Animam	
	May the Body and Blood of Christ Keep My Soul	179
69	Ut in Me Non Remaneat Macula	
	That no Stain of Sin May Remain in Me	185
70	Mortem Domini Annuntiabis	
	You Shall Show Forth the Death of the Lord	187
71	Divinitatis Tuae Sempiterna Fruitione	
	Grant Us, O Lord, That Eternal Enjoyment of Thy Godhead	189
72	Placeat Tibi Sancta Trinitas	
	May the Homage of My Service Be Pleasing to Thee, O Holy Trinity	191
73	Et Verbum Caro Factum Est	
	And the Word Was Made Flesh	193
74	Deo Gratias	
	Thanks Be to God	195

Epilogue

Ave Maria, Gratia Plena
Hail Mary, Full of Grace   197

THE LADDER

THE MYSTIC LADDER OF SANCTITY HAS ITS BASE IN THE SOUL'S "CONTRITION" FOR SIN; ITS STEPS ARE WROUGHT BY THE "ILLUMINATION" OF THE SPIRIT; ITS GOAL IS REACHED IN THE "UNION" OF THE WILL. FIRST, THE SOUL IS PREPARED AND STRENGTHENED; SECOND, IT MOUNTS CONFIDENTLY STEP BY STEP; THIRD, IT CASTS ITSELF ON THE VERY HEART OF GOD. THE HOLY MASS BODIES FORTH THIS ASCENT BY ITS LIFE-GIVING MYSTERIES. IT IS A WAY LEADING UPWARD TO GOD THROUGH HUMILITY, FAITH, AND LOVE. ONCE THE GOAL IS ATTAINED, ONE HAS BUT TO GIVE THANKS: HAS BUT TO BE, WITH CHRIST, A "EUCHARIST" TO GOD AND A PERPETUAL HOST.

CONTRITION OF THE SOUL

Quia Peccavi Nimis

CONTRITION IS THE VERY FOUNDATION UPON WHICH RESTS THE HOLY LADDER WHICH LEADS TO GOD. THIS CONTRITION PREPARES THE SOUL FOR ILLUMINATION IN FAITH AND UNION IN LOVE. IT FINDS EXPRESSION IN THE "PRAYERS AT THE FOOT OF THE ALTAR," WHICH FORM AN ACT OF PROFOUND HUMILITY.

I

IN NOMINE PATRIS ET FILII ET SPIRITUS SANCTI. AMEN.

IN THE NAME OF THE FATHER, AND OF THE SON, AND OF THE HOLY GHOST. AMEN.

A priest of Jesus Christ, consecrated for all eternity, I am the Ambassador of the Father, of the Son, and of the Holy Ghost. It is in the thrice-holy Name of a God so sublime, One and Three, that I, unworthy sinner that I am, approach this altar where His Majesty is throned.

I am the Envoy of Omnipotence, of infinite Wisdom, of boundless Love; I was anointed and consecrated to receive from the lips of the Most High the *Fiat* which I am soon to pronounce, the word which works the sublimest of miracles and divinely celebrates it.

Grace immeasurable, inconceivable, I have been given in order to make Oblation to God of Him Who is perfect God and perfect Man. Who only is Holy, Who only is Lord, Who only is Most High; in order to offer up Jesus Christ, the Incarnate Word, Son of God and Son of Man, blessed for ever and ever.

In the name of the Most Holy Trinity, Which predestined me to this purpose, and moved by a will which is wholly love, I am sent to promulgate this adorable decree to the people of God, to the holy people of God. It is I who shall offer today the oblations of this chosen people, itself clothed with a holy priesthood;[1] it is I, again, who shall receive from this God His bountiful gifts and distribute them to the people; I, also, who shall draw these souls irresistibly into the incomparable Sacrifice of Jesus Christ, shall envelop them therein, and, with them, become, with Him, and in Him, the Oblation pleasing to the ever Holy, ever Blessed, forever Adorable Trinity.

In the Name of this Trinity, in the Name of the Father, and of the Son, and

---

1 1 Pet. 2: 5.

of the Holy Ghost, that is, also, by virtue of, by the divine strength of this all-powerful Trinity, the only name of Which is Its own nature, I shall dare to mount the steps of the altar, pronounce there the most sacred formulas, and perform there the most solemn of rites. I, a clod of earth, drawn from the abyss of nothingness, I, born in sin like every child of Adam, shall hold in my creature hands infinite Purity and shall make thereof Oblation unto God; I shall bring Jesus Christ to the souls who hunger and thirst for the Life eternal that He is.

In what a mystery we are about to participate, I and this people surrounding me! We are about to pronounce Glory to the Name of the Father, and of the Son, and of the Holy Ghost; we shall be plunged, as it were, into this glory, *in Nomine.*[2] By the power of this Sacrifice, which is perfect worship of God, We shall be restored to our Father, to this God of Whom in baptism we were born, *qui ex Deo nati sunt.*[3]

In the Name, that is, again, to the glory of Oneness in Trinity, of Trinity in Oneness, we shall body forth the divine plan concerning us all: having become the Oblation of God in Jesus Christ, we shall have our being, live, and be consumed with love in His presence, like a holocaust, surrendering everything even to the very ashes. So shall we return into the fellowship of that divine Family which the grace of Jesus made so truly ours.

Thus each morning, with the family of God, particularly with that one especially confided to me by my priesthood, I shall be able to penetrate deeper and deeper into the *bosom of the Father where rests His only begotten Son,*[4] He Who from love of me, for my salvation, descended from Heaven and became, on the Cross and on the altar of His sacred Humanity, both Priest and Victim of the Sacrifice of the Saints.

Father, Son, Holy Spirit, I and all of us sign ourselves in honor of Thee with the sign of the Cross, with that Cross upon which, by Thy power, was accomplished one time to Thy glory this miracle which I, Thine Envoy, unworthy on every count, am about to renew *to the praise and glory of Thy holy Name, to our benefit, and to that of all Thy holy Church.*[5]

Amen. So be it! Yes, may it so be! I have no other intention in my mind, in my heart. That is why, even in all the confusion I feel at appearing in Thy

---

2 In Greek; accusative indicating motion into.
3 Who are born of God (John 1: 13).   4 John 1: 18.
5 *Suscipiat* of the Mass.

presence, yet also in the unshaken confidence that Thou wilt kindly receive and hear me, I dare entreat Thee, Holy Trinity, to accept even now this Sacrifice of Jesus Christ, in which I hide myself, myself and these faithful, all the souls whom for Thy sake I love.

Amen, Fiat, Deo gratias! By this Sacrifice shalt Thou be glorified, and once more the work of Thy Redemption will be wrought.... *Opus nostrae redemptionis exercetur!*[6] *So be it!*

---

6 The work of our redemption is wrought (*Secret* of the 9th Sunday after Pentecost).

II

INTROIBO AD ALTARE DEI

I WILL GO IN UNTO THE ALTAR OF GOD

I will go in unto the Altar of God, unto God Who giveth joy to my youth. How fruitful is this first thought which, at the beginning of the sacrifice, invites to deep contemplation the whole soul of a priest and the souls of the people who sacrifice with him!

The altar of stone there before his eyes is a symbol. And what a symbol! How arresting, how sacred, how sublime! The altar of God, the true altar of the thrice-holy God, art Thou Thyself, O Lord Jesus Christ; that altar is Thy sacred Humanity; *introibo ad altare Dei ad Deum.*[1] ... The altar of God is this God of God, become flesh to become this Altar, its Priest and its Victim; and so to remain, Priest and Victim, through endless ages!

A priest of Jesus Christ, I can not perform my dread functions in all sanctity without entering into this Altar of God, without becoming one with this *Rock* which is Christ,[2] without taking to myself His own fervor of spirit, His own intentions without desiring, with Him, to make His whole being and mine, body and soul, the altar of the awe-inspiring Sacrifice.

And I, likewise, merely one of the faithful approaching this Altar of God, must wish to become one with this *Rock* if I would put on Christ, if I would be in my mind and in my heart the altar whereon Jesus will be immolated and offered.

Today I mount to this Altar, to Jesus Christ, my Lord and my God; I enter into Him and with Him hide myself in God; stretched upon this *Rock*, I let the wounds of my crucified Saviour be imprinted deeply within me, wounds symbolized by the five great crosses hewn in the altar stone. Priest, victim, altar, with Him and through Him, so must I appear in the eyes of Holy Church if I would truly devote myself to the *Mystery of the great Ac-*

---

1 I will go in unto the altar of God, to God... 2 1 Cor. 10: 4.

tion[3] which renews the Oblation of Jesus Christ.

At this price alone will joyous exultation be mine; my youth will be renewed, revived; I shall recover that holy energy of past years, that fervor which at my ordination to the priesthood or at my First Holy Communion the Holy Spirit poured so abundantly into my soul, thirsting to be *likened to the Son of God and be thus a priest forever.*[4] That youth of exalted thoughts, of ardent desires, of love burning for action, that youth shall be renewed like the eagle's;[5] I shall feel my wings stronger now to bear me to divine heights. So, at the foot of the holy altar, a priest's soul is recreated, and so, too, every Christian soul if it but lose itself again willingly in Jesus, its Supreme Ideal.

Do thou remember, O my soul, those first-fruits offered in a past already dim! Remember what streams of faith and love Jesus thy Lord let rise in thee at that first approach to His altar, at that first contact with the *Rock* which is Himself—let rise and overflow the boundaries of thy being, to His glory, for the salvation of souls, for thine own sanctification! Oh, remember!...

Let me know again, O Christ Jesus, the joys of that first meeting! Let the nails of Thy blessed Passion pierce me ever deeper and more deep; renew in my innermost being that *Mystery of faith* and that experience of love. Let me be entirely Thy priest, standing like John, Thy beloved disciple, upright at the foot of Thy Cross, beneath the Tree of Life.

Let me enter into Thee! Let not my unworthiness too greatly repel Thee, and once within Thee, let me no more leave Thee forever! Unite my soul to Thy sacred soul, O Christ, that in Thee I may find again and guard with constancy my whole joy, the joy of my priestly youth, vivid as then!...

Come, let, us enter! Let us penetrate together into Jesus Christ! Let us hide in His Wounds, let us disappear within these walls that guard in God.

---

3 Ancient name for the Sacrifice of the Mass.
4 Heb. 7: 3.   5 Ps. 102: 5.

III

JUDICA ME, DEUS, FORTITUDO MEA

JUDGE ME, O GOD, THOU, MY STRENGTH

O Lord, my God, judge me, Thou, my Strength! For I am a sinner; Thou alone canst restore my soul.

Lo, I bear to the foot of Thine altar—altar which Thou art!—my innumerable sins, past and present, my outrages against Thy Majesty, my countless infidelities, my endless neglects. A load of death!

Like Thee, gentle Lamb of God, I carry also the sins of all this people surrounding me in this solemn hour, the sins of the whole world, crimes rising like a mountain before Thy Face. A fearful burden!

Judge me, judge us, but like a merciful Father Who forgives the prodigal son crying out to Him, *Pater peccavi,* Father, I have sinned against Heaven and before Thee![1] I wish not to be of the nation that is not holy, *de gente non sancta,* that forgets Thee, scorns Thee, transgresses Thy law, O mighty God! I will no longer be of this perverse age, the world of today that renounces its Christian dignity: I would live like Thy saints, with Thy saints, live as a saint of Christ!

Deliver me, heavenly Father, from the unjust and deceitful man, *ab homine iniquo et doloso,* from Satan, from whoever is determined to separate me from Thee. Tear me from the world, from the flesh, from the allurements of surrounding life, from all who would entice me to the broad way, th easy and open road that leads to all compromise, all weakness, all yielding.

Tear me, Lord, from the *fascinations of earthly pleasures,*[2] from vanity in every form. Let me not be like *the broken cistern, emptying itself through every crevice.*[3] Distinguish my cause, *discerne causam meam;* my cause is Thine, O just God!

---

1 Luke 15: 18.   2 Wis. 4: 12.   3 Jer. 2: 13.

For Thou, O God, art my strength, *tu es, Deus, fortitudo mea....* What courage that thought gives my soul at the dawn of a new day! Ah! yes, my vocation is great, beautiful, enviable on every count. But what responsibilities, what sacrifices, what struggles that vocation implies!

Whether priest or simple Christian, is it not my whole being that I have to give over to God each time I approach His altar? To live, is not that for me self-immolation?

To be man, only a man, yet live here below like the angels! To be a clod of earth, yet live like a spirit! To be nothing, yet destined to carry God!... Thou art my strength, my God! *In Thee have I hoped. I said: Thou art my God, my times are in Thy hands!*[4]

Thy strength, O Father, that strength which triumphs in me, is Jesus Christ, He, Thy Virtue, Thy Power, He, the adorable worker of Thy miracles in those whom Thou lovest, in Thy priests, in all of us, Thy faithful. Have pity on our weakness; cast us not off, abandon us not to despair, to that despair of life which overwhelms and would engulf us when the enemy—Satan, the Flesh, the World—harasses and defeats us. Let me not need to say today: *Quare tristis incedo, dum affligit me inimicus?*[5]

O Lord, I have confidence in Thy strength; I lean upon it, as on a lever that is to lift the incredible weight of my earth-bound soul. Thou art God, Thou are the Powerful, Thou art the Shield and Buckler of the saints; then do Thou defend me, the miserable sinner who cries to Thee in his extremity!

---

4 *Offertory* of the 13th Sunday after Pentecost.
5 Why go I sorrowful whilst the enemy afflicteth me?

IV

EMITTE LUCEM ET VERITATEM TUAM

SEND FORTH THY LIGHT AND THY TRUTH

Let Thy Light and Thy Truth descend.... Thy Light, O Father in Heaven, Thy Light of Light, true God of true God, that is Thine only begotten Son, Jesus, Thine Anointed, my Saviour, He Whom I desire to be *all in all things* for myself and for those I love, *omnia et in omnibus.* He is Thy Truth, as He is Thy Light. He is the radiance of Thine infinite Knowledge and the splendor thereof, radiance and splendor so perfectly identical with the Sun, with the Light which engenders them, that they are the Truth of God.

O Light, Truth descending from the invisible, inaccessible summits of the Father, I adore Thee, I thank Thee.... Thou art my God; my very intelligence, though weak and darkened by sin, is nevertheless an infinitesimal spark flown from the ardent heart of Thy Light and Truth. For that reason it adores Thee, humbling its pride before Thy Face; it gives Thee thanks for all the benefits which, despite its unworthiness, Thou dost bestow upon it, especially for the gift of faith with which Thou deignest to enlighten it. Let it return to Thee plenteously, unreservedly, to be united in entire joyousness with Thy Light and to bathe therein as in its proper element.

I cry to Thee, O Light, in this most solemn hour of my day as I bow low at the foot of Thine altar and confess my darkness. Light from the Father, scatter my darkness! Drive from my heart all that is of shadow, obscurity, night, that Thou mayest enter in! Between Thy light and my darkness, between Christ Who is Justice and myself, sinner, is no possible communion!...[1] O Lord Jesus, conquer the sinner!... *Emitte lucem tuam!*

Truth from the Father; shed upon me and upon all of us that lambent radiance that descended victorious upon Thy disciples on Thabor. Envelop

---

1 *Cf.* 2 Cor. 6: 14 (Translator's note).

us with Thy shining garment, white as the snow; enflame us with the divine fire that flows from Thy glorified Countenance!... *Emitte veritatem tuum!*

Truth without shadow, Wisdom without defect, Clearness without obscurity, establish us in truth, in justice, in purity. Come, Thou Light inextinguishable! Dispel our confusions, dissipate our lies, blot out all the falsehood of a life belonging not entirely and singly to God!

Take us by the hand, lead us, that we may go up to Thine altar and breathe forth our longing for the vision Thou dost promise us there—a vision purely of faith, yet even now revealing what glory! Only within Thee, O Light, shall we sometime see all Light and be inebriated with the torrent of Thy pleasure. *Torrente voluptatis tuae potabis eos ... et in lumine tuo videbimus lumen.*[2]

---

[2] Thou shalt make them drink of the torrent of Thy pleasure ... and in Thy light we shall see light (Ps. 35: 9 *ff.*).

V

IN MONTEM SANCTUM ET IN TABERNACULA TUA

UNTO THY HOLY HILL AND INTO THY TABERNACLES

Let Thy Light and Thy Truth lead me and bring me unto Thy Holy hill and into Thy tabernacles!... I am to ascend this hill today; in these tabernacles I must find repose. Thy hill, O Father, is Thy Son, Jesus Christ, and Thy tabernacles are His sacred wounds which we kiss in silent adoration.

I gaze longingly at Thy heights, my Saviour, Summit of God, Supreme Love, Pinnacle of life! I long to be separated from the crowd, tear myself from the earth, and attain to Thee, Thou highest Mountain, crown of all the hills of God, crown of Thy saints, in whom is glorified Thy justice. *Justitia tua sicut montes Dei.*[1]

Lord Jesus, eternal Beatitude, Master, Teacher of blessedness! I am consumed with desire to enjoy Thy happiness at last, O Happiness inexhaustible! Let me climb the Mount of Beatitudes which Thou art, where Thou revealest the secret of enjoying Thee and of enjoying all things in Thee!

Lord Jesus, Thabor still illumined by the fires of glory which dazzled Peter and James and John that day Thou appearedst to them, Thy Face shining like the sun, Thy garments white as snow! My God, Splendor of the Father, I long to abide forever in the radiance of Thy Visage—Beauty old, yet ever new, *Image of the invisible God!*[2]

Living Mount Calvary, Jesus crucified! I shall soon be with Thee: therein consists the entire peace of the soul; there is no other. I shall watch by Thy Cross, *juxta crucem*, beside Thee, like the good thief, whom Thou forgavest, promising him "this very day" Thy peaceful paradise. And I shall exult in Thee, in Thy Passion which I am about to commemorate, in Thy death which I am about to announce.

---

[1] Thy justice is as the mountains of God (Ps. 35: 7).   [2] Col. 1: 15.

Levavi oculos meos in montes,[3] yes, I have lifted up my eager eyes to these mountains, *O Mountain of God, fruitful Mountain wherein God is well-pleased to dwell.*[4] Draw me to Thee, Lord Jesus! Whether I be priest at Thy sacrifice or one of the faithful there present, let me mount to Thy heights; let no perishable, no earthly or transitory thing keep me from Thee! Give me the swift white wings of the dove; *Quis dabit mihi pennas sicut columbae, et volabo et requiescam?*[5]

When shall I come to Thy tabernacles?

Let me fly and rest in them, Lord, today! Let me hide in Thy sacred wounds, which Thou bearest forever glorious in Thy glorified Humanity, and which were opened in that blessed Passion, the mystery of which I am about to celebrate and commemorate.

Quam dilecta tabernacula![6] How lovely are Thy tabernacles, O Jesus! How they invite, allure, call forth devotion! With special joy and in the fullness of love, I contemplate the wide open wound in Thy holy side, the very one in which Thomas placed his hand, crying out, "My Lord and my God!"[7] Ah, what a tabernacle is that! How good it is to seek shelter there when I follow or cooperate in the great work of redemption being accomplished at the altar!

Wound in the side of Jesus, wonderful tabernacle of the holiness of my Lord and my God! I strain upward to Thee! I long to penetrate into this Sanctuary, into this Holy of Holies, and establish in it my dwelling, for *it is good, indeed, to be here!*[8]

Send forth, O Lord, Thy Light and Thy Truth; may they lead me and bring me unto Thy holy hill and into Thy tabernacles! There I shall meet Thy saints, all those who, like the Apostle, could cry out: *I bear the marks of the Lord Jesus in my body!*[9] Do Thou imprint those wounds at least in the very depths of my heart, that I may never more forget Thy love, Thy suffering, Thy sacrifice.

---

3 I have lifted up my eyes to the mountains (Ps. 120: 1). 4 Ps. 67: 17.
5 Who will give me wings like a dove, and I will fly and be at rest? (Ps. 54: 7).
6 Ps. 83: 2. 7 John 20: 28. 8 Matt. 17: 4 9 Gal. 6: 17.

VI

CONFITEBOR TIBI IN CITHARA

I WILL PRAISE THEE UPON THE HARP

I will praise Thee upon Thy Harp, my God, and I will hope.... Heavenly Father, in my confusion I wish to conceal myself from Thy gaze. I hide in the sacred Humanity of Thy beloved Son, in Whom Thou art well pleased.[1] I take His virtues, cover myself with them, let them pervade my being. I clothe myself with the virtues of the eternal Priest, the spotless Victim, the Altar sacrosanct. He is the divine Harp, the only one that gives Thee worthy praise, the only one whose ineffable unceasing canticle Thou delightest ever to hear.

In my sinful hands I take this Harp, this Heart of the God-man, and by it, in it, with it, I praise Thee today and cry out to Thee in the name of all souls: *Deus meus,* O my God! Hear with fatherly, merciful ear the triad of profound faith, invincible hope, and repentant love which rises for me and for them from Jesus Christ, the instrument of praise of Thy saints.

Harp of God, O Jesus Christ, resound, clamor, supplicate for us, for me—for me, miserable sinner, vile nothing, weakness inarticulate, uninspired!

Why art thou sad, O my soul, and why dost thou disquiet me? Quare tristis es? Can there be reason still for sadness and anxiety when one is being borne upward to God by the transcendent praise of Jesus Christ, in unison with the throbbing of His mighty Heart?

Spera in Deo, hope in God, hope in thy Priest, thy Victim, thine Altar! Hope in thy Redeemer, in the Sacrifice He will renew in a moment, the Sacrifice which is perfect worship, perfect thanksgiving, the only prayer which implores victoriously and which expiates....

Hope, priestly and Christian soul! Hope is the anchor of the saints. In

---

1 Matt. 3: 17.

Jesus Christ, the eternal Priest, thou hast cast thine anchor, in Him Who having returned to the Father reigneth at His right hand forever; verily thou hast cast thine anchor in the firm substance of God himself. Already, by right, if not in fact, thou reignest with Him, there where He dwelleth, where *He intercedeth constantly for His own, living only for that.*[2]

Hope, O my soul, for on the Harp of God, on Christ, I shall make hymns of praise here on earth; and in Heaven I shall praise on it eternally this Father Who so loveth us, *Who hath given us His only-begotten Son that henceforth we may live through Him alone.*[3]

Divine Harp of the saints, Lord Jesus Christ, I hope in Thee at this hour of the day, when I appear before Thy Father's Face! Thou art Thyself the salvation of my countenance, *salutare vultus mei*. With Thee, by Thee, in Thee, I can gaze toward Him; now, in all security, I can plunge my child-gaze into the eyes of my Heavenly Father; in all kindness He will look upon me and will say even of me: *Hic est filius meus dilectus, in quo mihi bene complacui.* This is my beloved Son in Whom I am well pleased.[4]

Salutare vultis mei et Deus meus[5] Thou art my God, O Jesus Christ! I give myself up anew, this very moment, to Thy priestly influence upon me; I thirst this morning to be invaded, penetrated, transformed by Thee! Let me enter into Thee, Thee my Altar, to renew there my youth, my strength, all the transports of those first days when, my hands still fragrant with the holy oil, I lifted up to Thee my heart and my whole being, Deus meus!... Do Thou remember that!

---

[2] Heb. 7: 25. [3] 1 John 4: 9. [4] Matt. 17: 5.
[5] The salvation of my countenance and my God...

VII

GLORIA PATRI ET FILIO ET SPIRITUI SANCTO

GLORY BE TO THE FATHER, AND TO THE SON,
AND TO THE HOLY GHOST

Glory be to the Father, and to the Son, and to the Holy Ghost! Glory be to Thee, O blessed Trinity, O highest Unity! Honor and glory be to Thee, O God, Who art Power, Wisdom, infinite Goodness!

I come to offer Thee Jesus Christ and, by Him, with Him, in Him, I come to offer mine own self as a *living oblation*. I would that it might be *holy and pleasing* in Thine eyes,[1] *an odor of sweetness;*[2] I would that it might be a cause of rejoicing to Thy Church and of service to Thy saints!

Today and every day of my life, my only desire is to glorify Thee. To that glory which is Thy sacred, divine life, that glory which Thou enjoyest in the ineffable relations which constitute Thee, O adorable Trinity, to that I can add nothing, eternal and essential Unity in Trinity, Trinity in Unity! I can only adore that glory, desiring that it may be always what it was, what it is now, what forever it must be, *Sicut erat ... et nunc ... et in saecula....*

But to Thine external glory, O ever tranquil and blessed Trinity, my sacrifice can and must add today that perfect homage which is due to Thee. For Thou, O Lord, hast created all things, Thou holdest dominion over them, claimest rightfully of Thy creatures—and this is peculiarly their own glory—their utter dependence in all ways upon Thee, and awaitest that they confess Thine absolute, sovereign, divine rights over them.

And therefore, to augment that glory ever susceptible of increase, I come to offer Thee Jesus Christ, the spotless Oblation, the Holocaust of holocausts that, through Him, I may bring Thee the homage of my nothingness, Thee, my Creator; that I may sacrifice that nothingness to Thee,

---

1 Rom. 12: 1.   2 Eph. 5: 2.

affirming thus my adoration, acknowledging Thine innumerable favors, crying out for help in my necessities, and imploring Thy grace and mercy in my weaknesses.

This oblation of Jesus which I make my own, will today be *Thy great glory;* it will restore Thy creature to Thee Who madest it, lovedst it, savedst it, to Thee Who desirest one day to crown it in the shining glories of the saints. For that I rejoice and *exult in my Saviour;* for it is the law of my nature, it is my true security, it is an inescapable urgency of my soul to acknowledge Thee thus, O Holy Trinity, my King, my Master, my God.

Amen. So may it ever be, my God! *Amen, Amen, Amen!* So it was in the beginning of all things, and even when as yet they were not: for all things praised Thee in the eternal ideas which already Thou didst have of them and which Thou art. So may it be now likewise and forever, in the timeless reaches of eternity! *Amen.*

VIII

ADJUTORIUM NOSTRUM IN NOMINE DOMINI

OUR HELP IS THE NAME OF THE LORD

Our help is in the Name of the Lord, Who made Heaven and earth. Once more, before going deeper into the knowledge of our misery, before being overcome by the sense of our guilt, we call upon the thrice-holy Name of God, Who created all things and made us His creatures.

The *Name of the Lord,* is it not in very truth Jesus Christ? As the divine and adorable expression of the perfections of God, it is embraced by the Father, penetrated by the Word, inundated with love by the Holy Spirit. *And for that cause the Name of Jesus Christ is a Name above all names; for that cause, as soon as it is pronounced, every knee bows, of those that are in Heaven, on earth, and under the earth, and every tongue confesses that Jesus Christ is in the glory of God the Father.*[1]

Name holy and terrible,[2] I cast myself to earth before Thee in adoration, "O Jesus Christ, O Jesus Christ, O Jesus Christ!"[3] I gaze at the Heavens, searching their infinite deeps; I contemplate the earth and its abysses; I see nothing so great as Thou, nothing so wise, nothing so powerful, nothing so sublime, so desirable as Thou, *Name of the Lord.* And I feel therefore an endless confidence in Thy help rise within my soul. Name of Jesus, be my help!

The renewal of the Work of Redemption, in which I cooperate this morning, is Thy Work, the Work of Thine infinite power and wisdom, of Thy supreme goodness. Deity alone could undertake it, accomplish it. How could man, dust and impotence that he is, dare appear before the Face of God, enter into discussion with His majesty, expect to find in His mercy the abundant salvation which is there? *Quia apud Dominum misericordia et copiosa apud eum redemptio.*[4]

1 *Cf.* Phil. 2: 9–11.   2 Ps. 110: 9.   3 Bossuet.
4 Because with the Lord there is mercy: and with Him plentiful redemption (Ps. 129: 7).

O Name blessed among all names, O Jesus Christ, *Great Pastor of the sheep,*[5] eternal High-priest of the saints, come to my aid, compensate superbly, triumphantly for my deficiencies! Incomparable Priest of God, I immerse my soul in Thy sanctity, I shield myself beneath Thy justice. Engulf my weaknesses, deliver me from my iniquities, wash away the defilement of my sins, and clothe me in the shining alb which Thou, O Lamb of God, madest white in the Precious Blood of our redemption.[6]

What can I not hope from Thy succor! *Thou hast made Heaven and earth.* Day and night the works of Thy hands vie with one another in praising the sublimity of their Creator; they confess His power. As for me, a grain of sand, an unknown atom in this vast structure of Thy goodness, *I have put my trust in Thee; I said, Thou art my hope, O God, my lots are in Thy hands.*[7] And I found new courage—that courage with which Thou ever fillest a contrite and humbled heart. Let the force of Thine own greatness of spirit be made manifest in me today, my God, that, following Thee, and upborne by Thy strength, I may go even *to the mountain of myrrh and unto the hill of frankincense.*[8]

What glory will revert thereby unto Thee, and with what festive garment wilt Thou cloak my destitution! Thy saints will be gladsome and will sing: *Thou art good, and Thy mercy endureth forever.*[9]

Help of God, of the Father, of the Son, of the Holy Spirit, most holy Name of Jesus Christ, spread out the pinions of Thy power and sweep down over us; cover our human misery with the healing shadow of Thy wings! Let it feel all the force of Thy influence; let it forget what it is, to remember henceforth only Thee! May it no longer be!... Thou art....

---

[5] Heb. 13: 20. [6] Apoc. 7: 14. [7] Ps. 30: 16.
[8] Cant. 4: 6. [9] Ps. 106: 1

IX

CONFITEOR QUIA PECCAVI

I CONFESS THAT I HAVE SINNED

I confess ... that I have sinned, through my fault, through my fault, through my most grievous fault. And as I so confess, I bow down low, longing to prostrate my nothingness before the All, before the Majesty of the Most Holy God which I have dared to offend....

Confiteor.... Methinks one should really say, *I praise Thee,* O my God, *I give Thee thanks.*[1] And, in very truth, as I here abase my misery, as I fain would let it mingle with the earth towards which I bow myself in humiliation, my intention in accusing myself is to praise the mercifulness of Him Who never better manifests His mercy than in pardoning.

I praise Thee, my God, Almighty God, Who canst punish me when I sin; Who hast spared me, unwilling to destroy the work of Thy hands; Who hast desired to give Thy creature time to repent, to amend; Who, having permitted his sin, art strong enough to draw therefrom a greater good, Thee I praise and I bless, Almighty God!

Borne down in my nothingness, I abase myself, fall at Thy feet.... *O look upon me and have mercy on me,*[2] *Thou Who forsakest nothing that Thou hast made, Thou Who overlookest the sins of men for the sake of repentence; Who forgivest them because Thou art the Lord our God.*[3] I praise Thee, good God, Who wilt not that we perish, *Who hast mercy, because Thou art the Powerful.*[4]

I praise thee, O Mary, Virgin of Virgins, Immaculate Conception which in prevision of the redeeming blood of Jesus, could not be sullied by the impure lava of original sin.... Advocate of sinners, I bless thee, for if I return to my God, O Mediatrix, is it not always owing to thee?

I praise thee, blessed Michael Archangel, first of the faithful, of those who, at the *non serviam* of Lucifer and his hosts, flourished the standard of submis-

---

1 Real meaning of the Latin word, *Confiteor.*
2 Ps. 85: 16.   3 Wis. 11: 24.   4 *Ibid.*

sion, making Heaven to ring with their rallying cry; *Quis ut Deus?* —Who is like God?

I praise thee, blessed John the Baptist, greatest of those born of women, example of penitence, perfect model of austerity, of self-control, of chastity; martyr, first witness for innocence!

I praise you, blessed Apostles Peter and Paul, immovable pillars of the Church, God's incomparable penitents, who could but answer Jesus simply, as didst thou, Peter—*Lord Thou knowest all things, Thou knowest that I love Thee,*[5] and as thou didst, Paul—Who art Thou, Lord; and what wilt Thou have me to do?[6]

I praise you, all God's Saints, you who have tasted the gift of tears and who obtain it for all who desire to wash away their offenses in the waters of contrition.

I praise thee, my Father, thou Father of my soul, who often hearest it, who ever grantest it pardon, who drawest it to the altar of God, there to renew its youth.... And you, *my brothers* here present, witnesses of my offenses but also of my sorrow.... Saints of God, *I praise you,* all, many as you are; I praise you, I thank you.... Ye obtain for me this *contrite and humbled heart,* the most pure offering which will appease the Lord, Whom I have so offended—yea, so outraged—so many times have I turned from Him to the love of creatures, forgetting that I am made for God alone, my supreme goal.... Quia peccavi nimis cogitatione, verbo et opere....[7]

Mea culpa, mea culpa, mea maxima culpa.[8] My perverse thoughts pass before my eyes; I number my offending words; I recoil before my misdeeds; and I see that it was my fault, yes, my fault alone, my most grievous fault, that thus I have heaped ingratitude upon ingratitude....

O Blessed Mary, O all ye Saints of God, pray, *pray to the Lord our God for me!* Misery, nothingness, implores you, beseeches you; yet also goodwill supplicates you; *ideo precor:*[9] move Him to look mercifully upon me in this most solemn hour, in order that, purified in the tears of Jesus, in thine, O Mary, in the tears of all the saints, and in mine own, I may serve at this pure sacrifice, the only one that fully pleases and perfectly praises Him. *Confiteor.*

---

5 John 21: 17.   6 *Cf.* Acts 9: 5–6.
7 For I have sinned exceedingly, in thought, word and deed....
8 Through my fault, through my fault, through my most grievous fault.
9 Therefore I beseech.

X

DEUS, TU CONVERSUS VIVIFICABIS NOS

THOU SHALT TURN AGAIN, O GOD, AND QUICKEN US

O God, if Thou turn toward us, Thou wilt quicken us.... Only the glance of God, which penetrates to the very depths of a soul, can so renew, increase, and enrich its life. *My God, look upon me and have mercy on me!* [1]

Real sorrow for sin, contrition heavy with tears—such tears as soften the arid wasteland of my heart—that contrition should be nothing other than a loving looking upward of my soul to God, a look of unshakable confidence, a look that affirms: *My God, I trust myself to Thee, for I am sure of Thee.* Such a look is always answered by the Father of mercies, by the God of all consolation.

Who can estimate the divine effect of God's gaze upon a contrite and humbled soul that opens wide to His light, that drinks its fill of His ardor! A soul which is crushed beneath this purifying action, which moved by grace, has willingly renounced its pride—such a soul is like softened wax: God, at His pleasure, can imprint His image there, can impress thereon more and more clearly His divine features. This soul lives as never before, that is to say, it partakes more fully of the Truth, of the Love of its God; itself nothing, it has met with the All, and there can but result a more intense union between the Creator and His creature. *Deus, tu conversus, vivificabis nos.* [2]

This meeting and this union are a cause of rejoicing for the people of God; for a soul never benefits alone by them: the entire City of God perceives therefrom a salutary influence. Always from a contrite and humble soul there is wafted a lingering perfume of grace; a secret virtue goes out from it, as once from Jesus, a virtue that heals other wounds besides. Weak and infirm that we are, it seems that the proximity of a soul which is able humbly to confess its fault gives increase to our own confidence. Feeling

---

[1] Ps. 85: 16.   [2] Thou shalt turn again, O God, and quicken us.

ourselves no longer alone before the supreme Judge, we begin to expect from Him what is always to be hoped for from a Father. *Et plebs tua laetabitur in te.*³

Father of mercies, I, too, implore Thy pity, the pity Thou dost promise me in Jesus Christ, Thine everlasting mercy. Manifest it to us, to me; show it to all who know the *plentiful redemption*⁴ that is in Him and the salvation that will not end. *Ostende nobis ... misericordiam ... et salutare da nobis.*⁵

To Thee I utter my prayer; to Thee I send up my cry. O let this cry that breaks forth from my soul in hope come unto Thee, to Thee Who repulsest never the humble suppliant.... *et clamor meus ad te veniat!*⁶

---

3 And Thy people shall rejoice in Thee. 4 Ps. 129: 7.
5 Show us Thy Mercy. And grant us Thy salvation.
6 And let my cry come unto Thee.

XI

DOMINUS VOBISCUM

THE LORD BE WITH YOU

May the Lord be with you and abide with you!... May He be with thee and abide with thee, Priest of Jesus Christ, *Et cum spiritu tuo....* I stretch out my hands, longing for God, possessed with a burning desire to climb this *mountain of myrrh*, this *hill of frankincense*[1] which is the altar, whence flow immeasurable graces for the faithful who are here, and for my soul in particular. *Dominus vobiscum.*

The Lord be with you! Beautiful and profound prayer! Two words only, yet they hold fathomless deeps of grace. This prayer is essentially a message of peace, of reconciliation, of love. It rises like a jet of flame to the throne of infinite Mercy, to the feet of God, before Whom I have just abased myself, confessing my sins, Whom I adored in my lowliness—in my nothingness, which, in the presence of the All-Powerful, sees itself in truth as very nothing.

Today again the Lord has pardoned me; He grants pardon to all of us. It is His answer to our humiliation for never does He repulse the contrite and humble heart, no, nor ever will! Rather does He stoop low to the sinner; tenderly He draws him to Himself, takes him in His arms, to His Heart, and gives him the kiss of peace. That pledge will be given me in a moment when I kiss the altar *Rock*, that likeness of Jesus, I shall remember it every time in the Holy Mass that, with the same rite, I repeat to the people surrounding me this aspiration after peace: The Lord be with you—*Dominus vobiscum;* every time the response comes for myself from their lips: The Lord be with thy spirit—*et cum spiritu tuo.*

The Lord be with us and abide with us! The most precious of all graces is *to be always with the Lord;*[2] that will be the endless joy of Heaven; oh,

---

1 Cant. 4: 6.   2 1 Thes. 4: 16.

may it, in anticipation of the eternal union, be also the gladness of earth!

Be with me, O my God! The soul to which Thou revealest Thyself, to which Thou showest somewhat of Thine infinite loveliness, when Thou grantest it forgiveness and, bending near, imprintest on its lips the divine seal of union,[3] that soul knows evermore no other happiness.

Abide in me that I may abide in Thee! So dost Thou invite me likewise in Thy holy Gospel, assuring me that only as I am united to Thee may my prayer be heard and I bear fruit, even in abundance![4] Then hold me fast in Thee whenever my weakness, my malice, would draw me away from this union, well-spring of peace. Let me never be separated from Thee; for, "O Lord Jesus, source of all beauty, where am I when I am not with Thee?"[5]

Abide with us all, that in Thee we may be but one heart, one soul, that the turbulent force of our will may flow away into Thine, and that Thy will may be done on earth as in Heaven, on the earth of our nothingness, as in the Heaven of Thy glory.

Stay with us, because it is towards evening, and the day is now far spent;[6] *already the shadows fall,*[7] and Thou approachest, Lord Jesus, *to render to every man according to his works.*[8] Do not abandon us in the hour every day announced in Thy Sacrifice, in that supreme hour, when we shall pass from the darkness of this valley of tears into the wondrous light of Thy divine splendor. *Mane nobiscum Domine!*[9]

---

3 *Cf.* Cant. 1: 1. 4 John 15: 4 *ff.* 5 St Anselm. 6 Luke 24: 29.
7 Cant. 4: 6. 8 Apoc. 22: 12. 9 Stay with us, Lord.

XII

OREMUS

LET US PRAY

Let us pray!... I stretch forth my hands as if actually to lay hold on God, for Whom my soul longs; then I join them again as if already inclasping the pledge of His infinite goodness—Himself; and I say: Let us pray—*Oremus.*

How many times this exclamation, this call to prayer, will recur in the course of the Sacrifice: *Oremus*—Let us pray!... Is not this Sacrifice the great prayer of prayers in which all others are merged? Is it not Thy prayer, O Jesus Christ, and therefore the divine prayer, since through it and in it Thou Thyself, eternal Priest, perpetual Victim, offerest Thyself again and ever again to Thy Father and offerest us together with Thee?

I stretch out my hands towards Thee, Lord Jesus; I will hold Thee, I do hold Thee fast, for I stand in need of Thee, in exceeding need of Thee and of Thy prayer, that I may go up unafraid to the altar of God and let my soul ascend unto Him.

I join them again; one might say I keep fast hold of Thee, possessing Thee, even as Thou possessest me. For Thou dost so possess me that in joining my hands Thou bindest them, that I may be as if delivered up to Thy sole power in the very moment when my weakness abandons itself in all confidence and security to Thee, O Jesus Christ!

Oremus, yes, let us pray, my brothers! Let our souls strive to reach Jesus; let us shut ourselves securely within Him; let us allow ourselves to be bound fast by the Force of God, by Jesus. Ah! How powerful will be our prayer, how living! For it is God Himself Who with you and with me, His minister, is about to pray to God.

Oremus—Let us pray. We are not alone at the foot of this Altar; the entire Church of God is in her sublime Priest, in her Christ. It is well with her there, borne as she is by Him, lifted up in the ascent of Thabor, of the hill of Calvary....

XIII

AD SANCTA SANCTORUM

INTO THE HOLY OF HOLIES

Take away from us our iniquities, we beseech Thee, O Lord, that we may be able to enter with pure minds into the Holy of Holies.... In order that we may penetrate therein, cleanse us from our misdeeds....

The *Holy of Holies* is the altar stone, that marble which is but the consecrated symbol of Jesus Christ, Priest, Victim, Altar of the Church of God. He it is to Whom I long to come; into Him I cry for entrance, in order that, clothed with His spirit, I may offer to Almighty God the oblation which will acknowledge His unrestricted, sovereign rights over me.

The *Holy of Holies* is Jesus Christ. He is sanctity itself; He is infinite purity, the God-man, with all the perfections which are His by virtue of His divine nature, together with those which human nature, through its ineffable union with the Word, confers upon Him and assures to Him for all eternity.

The *Holy of Holies* is Jesus Christ with His saints, whose sublime Head He is; Jesus Christ with the sanctity of all His members, His holy people, whose holiness is theirs only by virtue of His own holiness; with His saints, incomparable radiations of His own sanctity: facets, so to speak, of this Diamond, this precious Stone which He is, facets endlessly multiplied and flashing back the many-colored beams of His every glory, causing Him to be proclaimed the source and beauty of all sanctity.

The *Holy of Holies* is He, with the saints whose relics are enclosed here, walled into the altar stone as in the consecrated sepulcher which keeps them for the Life eternal; sheltered, as it were, in the adorable wound in His blessed side.

O Christ Jesus, Saint of saints, Priest, Victim, Altar, infinite sanctity, perfection of Thy saints, by Thy mercy, *by the merits of Thy saints*, whose relics are here sepulchred, forgive me all my sins!

Lovingly I kiss this altar stone which represents Thee. In so doing, like Mary of Magdala, the sinner who was the conquest of Thine unexampled love, I kiss the wounds in Thy sacred feet; would that, like her, too, I might wash them with a flood of tears—these wounds that shed the Precious Blood, ransom of all the souls that place their hope therein!

Wounds of Jesus, wounds of His divine feet, O let that blood flow, let it flow afresh upon my impurities; cleanse, sanctify, save my soul! Let sorrow break my stony heart, this *arid land*, this *waterless desert*,[1] that the gentle rain of Thy grace may sink into it and revive my soul. Give me of those graces that crowned Thy saints, all the holy priests who ever lived and who now live; Thy saints, of whom none dares to go up to Thine altar before his heart has been filled with grief for his sins.

By Thy tears, O God Who hast wept, by the tears of Mary and of Thy saints, forgive me, purify me, sanctify me, *O Holy of Holies! Then shall Thy light rise up in my darkness.*[2]

---

1 Ps. 62: 3.   2 Isa. 58: 10.

ILLUMINATION OF THE SPIRIT

Credo

BY ILLUMINATION THE SOUL MOUNTS ONE BY ONE THE STEPS OF THE LADDER THAT LEADS TO GOD. THE LIGHT OF FAITH REVEALS TO IT THE MYSTERY OF JESUS, PLUNGES IT THEREIN AND PREPARES IT FOR THE DELIGHTS OF THE APPROACHING UNION IN LOVE THIS ASCENT IS MADE FROM THE "INTROIT" TO THE "OFFERTORY".

XIV

CIBAVIT EOS[1]

HE FED THEM

In the form of a wondrous Sacrament, we offer to the Holy Trinity the Sacrifice which adores It and gives It thanks, which supplicates It and satisfies Its justice. In truth, when this great God has been conciliated, when His loving-kindness has called us to His arms, it is fitting that we should share in the divine Banquet. There, with Him, we shall enter into Communion with a Victim which, in giving Him all glory, grants to us complete forgiveness.

God, infinite in mercy, will give us as food—God, the Son of God, the Word Incarnate, the Word become the adorable Sacrament of the Eucharist. Down from His holy rood shall we take Him, even Jesus, or, if you will, in His glory we shall receive Him; and He, *Wheat* of the elect, will feed us with the *fat* of the ear; He, the *Rock* of promise, will give us our fill of that honey which possesses all sweetness.

Cibavit eos ex adipe frumenti;[2] yes, He fed His own with the fat of the wheat. He, the Wheat made into the *Bread of Life,*[3] He, the Word come down from Heaven into the earth of His sacred Humanity, humbled Himself there, emptied Himself of His glory; become man and crushed in His Humanity, He made Himself the pure Flour, the Bread of Sacrifice which alone is pleasing to His Father; and we, if we will, having offered it to this Father, Who is also ours, may consume it with the *fat,* that is to say, with the divine *force,* gift of the Holy Ghost, which is contained therein. This force which is God Himself diffuses itself through our powers, invades the substances of our souls, transforms them, and makes of them the very heads of the sheaf which Jesus wishes ground, which He desires to be, with Him,

---

1 Mass of the Feast of *Corpus Christi*, which is the subject of our *Meditations.*
2 He fed them with the fat of wheat (*Introit* of *Corpus Christi*).
3 John 4: 48.

the Bread of Sacrifice for the glory of His Father.

Et de petra melle saturavit eos. He filled them with honey out of the *Rock*. Thou, O Jesus Christ, are the spiritual *Rock*[4] which love smote and made its Victim. So smiting, this love opened the wide, gaping wound which lays bare Thy Heart. And the *honey* flowed broke forth from the cleft in a torrent—a Precious Blood which showed us how deep was Thy love for us, how deep was Thy love for Thy priest, all unworthy though he be. And this *Honey* of God, this most holy fluid, is become to me fullness of joy. I have found therein a new gift of the Holy Spirit—Piety, a gift of unspeakable sweetness which expands my soul and sends it running fearlessly along the ways of God. Thy ways, Lord Jesus, ways known and sought by Thy saints.

O Wheat of God, enter into my soul; yield me Thy most hidden, Thy most secret treasures! Feed my soul with the purest of Thy Being's substance, with the essence of its strength; give it of the *fat* of Thy vigor, that power which creates in whoever receives it those heroic virtues which enable Thy saints to dare great things for Thy glory.

Rock immovable, against which the enemies of God and of my soul but shatter their forces, let me come near to Thy Wound. Make the *Honey* of the Spirit to flow to my lips, to my heart; let this gift of piety recreate within me holy charity and keep me, child of the Father, entirely sheltered in His loving-kindness.

---

4 1 Cor. 10: 4.

XV

KYRIE ELEISON

LORD, HAVE MERCY

O Lord, we are overwhelmed by Thy Greatness, Thy Goodness, Thy Mercy. Once more let our nothingness cry out to Thee: *Have mercy, mercy on us, mercy on me!* Thou art Father; have mercy on Thy child! Thou art Son; have mercy on Thy brother! Thou art Love, O Holy Spirit; have mercy on my soul, Thy bride! O God, One in three Persons, have mercy on us, mercy on me!...

Kyrie eleison! Father, to Thee, sublime Fountain of the adorable Trinity, Creator of all things, Whom alone we must adore, to Thee, to Thy glory, must my worship be directed and, within this worship, the august Sacrifice of Thy well-beloved Son which I shall offer to Thee. Have mercy on me! *Kyrie eleison.*

In this hour I am conscious as never before of my abysmal nothingness, of my unspeakable unworthiness in presence of Thy Majesty.... I, nothing before the All; weakness before the All-Powerful; ignorance before the All-Wise; the finite before the Infinite; an atom before Immensity.... O measureless God, infinite Father, have mercy on me!... *Kyrie eleison.*

Christe eleison! Eternal Word, Son of the Father, Consubstantial with Him, Infinite, Measureless, All-Wise, All-Powerful like Himself, I adore Thee, I bless Thee, and my heart sinks in Thy presence. I am nothing; but in Thee and through Thee, Word Incarnate, O Christ, Priest of the Father, Mediator of men, Victim for sin, in Thee, through Thee, this my lowliness is lifted up: so transformed is it into worth that Thou wilt even have it to dwell within Thee and Thyself in it—this nothing! Have mercy on me!... *Christe eleison.*

Have mercy, stretch forth Thy hand to me, make me worthy to offer this Sacrifice, to be offered with Thee; prepare me for this priestly function which I am about to exercise to the glory of Thy Father, for the salvation of men! For all this, what detachment of soul I have need of! What purity, what charity! Oh, who will lift me above myself, if not Thou? Lord Jesus, have mercy on me!... *Christe eleison.*

Kyrie eleison! Holy Spirit of the Father and of the Son, eternal Kiss of the One and of the Other, bond of Their union, and, in Them, of all unions of earth and Heaven, have mercy on me!... *Kyrie eleison.*

God of Love, source of all charity, Thou Who didst espouse my soul in holy Baptism, Who gavest it as dower Thine own Gift, with the justice which likens me to Jesus Christ! O God, all-powerful Agent of this sublime Sacrifice, by virtue of which Thou desirest to flood my soul with the saving power of the Redemption, to saturate it with divine graces destined to make it, and keep it, holy, all holy, inviolate; have mercy on me, Lord, *Kyrie eleison.*

God of mercy, of all compassion, Father, Son, Holy Spirit, I surrender myself to Thee in this moment; I abandon myself to Thy secret and triumphant force. Work Thy mystery within me; redeem me ever and again at this Thine altar, before which I cast all my wretchedness, yet confidently, great God, with a soul full of trust in Thee, because it is sure of Thee! *Kyrie eleison.*

XVI

GLORIA DEO, PAX HOMINIBUS

GLORY BE TO GOD, PEACE TO MEN

Glory be to God on high, and on earth peace to men of good will. Is not this the perfect fruit of the holy Mass? Is it not the goal of this sublime Sacrifice? To give glory to God, to bestow peace on men—why, it is the whole Work of the Redemption, of the saving and sanctification of the human soul!

Gloria in excelsis Deo.... So sang the angel choirs in heavenly harmonies above the manger of the Holy Child; and since that time, through Jesus Christ, with Him, and in Him, the earth sends up to the Father, to the Son, and to the Holy Ghost, to Trinity in sacred Unity, the incense of its praise, the gold of its love, the myrrh of its oblations.

Glory be to God. That is the Holy Mass in its entirety, because, as Sacrifice, it is the confession of the absolute dominion of God over all creation; moreover, the adoration it calls forth, the plenteous thanksgivings it voices, the petitions it offers, the expiations it consecrates, all are homage to the glory of God, to that glory He conceives, of Himself, Father, Son, Holy Spirit, in the bosom of Their communications or ineffable relations, to that glory which we hallow—but also to that glory which all creation must offer Him, since indeed it came into existence principally for that. *Laudamus te, benedicimus te, adoramus te, glorificamus te, gratias agimus tibi, propter magnam gloriam tuam!*[1] Yes, for Thy great glory we thank Thee, O Holy Trinity, for that glory without eclipse which Thy boundless mercy received from Jesus the Redeemer, Thy Priest and Thy Victim, when, as messenger of peace to Thy creatures, He willingly made oblation of Himself upon the Cross, an oblation graciously to be renewed upon the altar.

---

1 We praise Thee; we bless Thee; we adore Thee; we glorify Thee. We give Thee thanks for Thy great glory.

Et in terra pax hominibus bonae voluntatis.[2] The delicious fruit of the Holy Mass is the peace it leaves in the hearts of men. Thou art this peace, Lord Jesus,[3] yes, Thou, with all that Thou art, all that Thou hast, all that Thou canst, all that Thou wilt. Thee, Peace of the Father, of the Son, of the Holy Ghost, Thee the Holy Sacrifice causes to descend into our souls—into my soul athirst for this Peace.

O Peace, O Jesus, Thou art my sweet Peace, that Peace which the world can as little offer as wrest from me. Thou art the Peace of men, of all who are single of heart, who seek the glory of God, and who make of their life a sacrifice, a complete holocaust, in which they will allow no robbery, even the least.[4]

On holy Good Friday, in the hour of the great and unique Sacrifice, Thou declaredst Thyself King of this Peace which Thou art when, after *fastening to the Cross the handwriting of the decree that was against us, which was contrary to us,*[5] Thou didst let Thy redeeming Blood flow over it and blot it out, didst wash us in that divine stream, and didst restore us to the glory of the Triune God.

Peace of the Father, Jesus, my Lord, deliver me utterly into the power of this Father, that thereby I may be created anew, in Thee! Peace of the Son, Jesus, my Lord, let me be reborn in that holy baptismal grace which grafted me on Thee and made me Thy brother, in Thee! Peace of the Holy Ghost, Jesus, my Lord, consume me in the ardor of Love which Thou art, that I may yield myself up entirely to God, to His glory, in Thee!

Glory be to God, peace to men who desire both the one and the other; that is the aim of the Holy Mass, to call forth this praise, to give freely of this peace to whoever pants for the waters that quench the thirst of the soul and bear it onward to eternal life.

---

2 And on earth peace to men of good will.
3 Eph. 2: 14.   4 Isa. 61: 8.   5 Col. 2: 14.

XVII

SUSCIPE DEPRECATIONEM

RECEIVE OUR PRAYER

Lord Jesus, Thou art the Mediator, *the only Mediator between God Thy Father and us;*[1] Thou art the Priest of our sacrifice, *the great Priest according to the order of Melchisedech;*[2] Thou art the *high Priest Who hast passed into the Heavens;*[3] and there, at the right hand of the Father, in all the glory of the *eternal Redemption by Thee obtained,*[4] in the midst of the splendors of divinity, Thou, true minister of the Holies[5] exercisest for us Thy sovereign and ever-during ministry.

Suscipe deprecationem nostram. Oh, receive our prayer! Receive this matchless *Prayer,* the Holy Mass;[6] take up from Thine altars this prayer pleasing to Thy heavenly Father, O Thou Who art Priest, Victim, and very Altar thereof in Thy blessed Humanity!

Holy Humanity of Jesus, Thou alone canst pray powerfully, victoriously, for us. Thou hast only to show to Thy Father those glorious scars which Thou still bearest, which Thou wilt bear resplendent in Heaven for all eternity, and which remain the inviolable pledges of our salvation.

This is in very truth the Holy Mass: Here below we offer Thee in sacrifice upon the earthly altar. The Church, Thy consecrated priests, all the faithful whom Baptism has clothed with a mystic, yet real, priesthood, all together, in Thee, we immolate Thee, Lord; and above, in high Heaven, before the Face of God, in the presence of His sublime Majesty, Thou appearest for us, pleadest for us, with the full power of Thine incomparable Sacrifice which perfects the elect in glory!

Suscipe deprecationem nostram. This morning I desire as never before to take refuge in Thy Prayer; I hide there, hide in *Thy Face,* O Jesus, which in

---

1 1 Tim. 2: 5. 2 Heb. 5: 6. 3 *Ibid.* 4: 14. 4 *Ibid.* 9: 12.
5 *Ibid.* 8: 2. 6 The most ancient name of the Mass. See *Notes sur la liturgie.*

that heavenly glory *shineth like the sun in his power,*[7] the while Thy Father, bending toward it, gives it for us the kiss of Peace, of reconciliation, of love.

For Thou only art Holy, *tu solus Sanctus.* Thy holiness is God's holiness; before it the very Seraphim veil their faces with their fiery wings, unable to bear its crowned glory....

For Thou only art Lord, O Jesus Christ, *tu solus Dominus.* Thou art the only-begotten Son, the Lord God, Son of the Father, consubstantial with Him, God of God, Light of Light, true God of true God. Thy prayer is God's own prayer to God.... My soul loses itself in this truth, ravished by its sublimity....

For Thou only art Most High, Lord Jesus, *tu solus altissimus, Jesu Christe!* Ah, receive my prayer today! Be Thou Thyself my whole prayer, Thou, Priest, Victim, Altar of my Sacrifice. Bear me upward on the soaring pinions of Thy flight divine, bear me high and far, ever higher, ever farther, away from every creature, though it were the very Seraph who swings before the Face of God the golden censer wherein are the burning prayers of the saints; though it were even those seven spirits of God who, lost in adoration before His throne, cease not to cry out: *Sanctus, Sanctus, Sanctus, Domine Deus....*[8]

Suscipe deprecationem nostram. Bear my prayer up to Thy throne in the place of Thy Majesty, holy Humanity of my Lord Jesus, there where, by right if not in fact, Thy glorious ascension *hath made me to sit beside Thee,*[9] in order to unite me with Thy Prayer....

7 Apoc. 1: 16.   8 Holy, Holy, Holy, Lord God....   9 Eph. 2: 6.

XVIII

DEUS, QUI NOBIS

O GOD, WHO TO US

O God, Who in this wondrous Sacrament hast left us a memorial of Thy Passion....[1] Such is the prayer which for centuries the Church has uttered to Jesus Christ when she desires to announce the dogma, the moral, the imperishable fruit of the Holy Eucharist, when she affirms her faith in this Sacrament, in this Sacrifice in which God Himself is immolated, offered up, and given as food to those who make themselves priests and victims with Him.... Ah, what a prayer!

Deus qui nobis.... O God Who hast left *us* this gift!... *Deus*, O God! To Thee I turn therefore in prayer, to Thee, eternal Son of the Father, consubstantial with Him, true God of true God! Also to Thee, O God-Man, to Thee, Eucharistic God, Body and Blood of Jesus Christ, my act of faith, rises today!

Most Holy Eucharist, adoring Thee thus objectified, I believe and confess that Thou art Jesus Christ and therefore God, *Deus!* All that I affirm—and would affirm if need be with my blood—of the Incarnate Word, I now affirm of the Word become Sacrament. Thou hast from the first moment all the dignity, grandeur, and sublimity of Jesus Christ! I see that Thou art important as He, necessary as He, worthy of the same praise as He, of the same veneration, of the same devotion, of the same adoration both from angels and men.

Divine Eucharist, Thou art not simply a sign, a figure, a dim appearance; Thou art not simply the instrument, the intermediary, the grace, or the gift of Jesus; Thou art Jesus Christ Himself, *God Who is blessed forever.*[2]

Deus, O God! Eucharistic God, Thou art He Whose Name is holy and

---

1 Collect of *Corpus Christi*. This and the following Meditation are inspired to a certain extent by the study of the Rev. Fr Albert Tesnière: *Somme de la prédication eucharistique*.
2 Rom. 1: 25.

terrible; the God of Majesty Whom the Angels praise, Whom the Dominations adore, Whom the Powers, trembling, revere....

Deus, O God! Eucharistic God, Thou art the God of glory Whom the Heavens and the Virtues of Heaven, the blessed Seraphim, praise in their ecstatic transports, because Thou art Jesus Christ, Who only is Holy, Who only is Lord, Who only is Most High and ever adorable. O God, *Deus!* I so believe.

Deus qui nobis.... O God Who to *us....* Yes, Thou givest Thyself thus to us, to me, O Eucharistic God.... What a contrast, almost I might say what a contradiction between these two words which the Church, our Teacher, places together in this way! *Deus qui nobis!*

On the one hand, O Holy Eucharist, Thou touchest what is most sublime, art Thyself that Sublimity; on the other, Thou abasest Thyself to what is most lowly; God and man. *Deus, nobis,* power and weakness, all and nothing, holiness and sin.... But there! *Too greatly hast Thou loved me, propter nimiam charitatem suam.*[3] Ah, yes, to excess, *nimiam charitatem,* with love exceeding great....

Already it was an excess of love to have made Thyself, O Jesus Christ, my companion in exile, *Se nascens dedit socium.*[4] Another excess was it that Thou madest Thyself my ransom by Thy death, *Se moriens in pretium.* Another—ah, and what an excess!—that Thou desiredst one day in Thy Kingdom to be my recompense, *Se regnans dat in praemium!* And could I ever have imagined that as pledge of all these excesses Thou wouldest add that of becoming the very food of my life, *Se convescens in edulium?*

Bread of my life, Thou givest me in Thy bounty an infinite gift containing all others, even the gift of Heaven, in the journey to which Thou art my viaticum, and of which Thou art the foretaste in joys too poignant for the human heart to bear.

O Jesus, Sacred Host, Thou art the Companion of my exile, my Sacrifice, the Giver of my guerdon; Thou wilt be in addition the Bread of my soul anhungered for Truth, athirst for Love; the Bread which is both a

---

3 For His exceeding charity (Eph. 2: 4).
4 Strophe of the hymn of the Most Blessed Sacrament at *Lauds* on *Corpus Christi*, of which the verses, numbered in the order given are: 1. In birth, man's fellow-man was He: 4. His meat, while sitting at the board; 2. He died, his ransomer to be; 3. He reigns, to be his great reward.

remedy in this world and a pledge of the world to come. And that for each one, from the smallest child who believes in Thee, to the exhausted old man impatient for Heaven; for the poor as for the rich; for the ignorant, for the scholar, for whoever desires to live a good life that he may die a good death.... *Propter nimiam charitatem suam.* Yes, too greatly hast Thou loved us!... *Deus qui nobis.*

I do not understand, do not see—I can not unite these two terms, can not bridge the chasm between them, *Deus—nobis.* But what matter! I do believe, Lord Jesus: Thou art the *Bread which giveth Life to the world.*[5]

---

[5] John 6: 52.

XIX

SUB SACRAMENTO MIRABILI

IN A WONDERFUL SACRAMENT

The ineffable means which God uses in His exceeding great love to give Himself thus to His unworthy creature is a Sacrament, a *wonderful Sacrament*, that is, a thing that contains holiness within itself, a hidden holiness; a cause capable of producing holiness; all that is a sign and symbol of holiness.[1]

By all these claims, O God Who thus givest Thyself so completely to us, this means which Thou art, O Eucharistic God, is a *Sacrament*, a *wonderful Sacrament*, it is the Sacrament supreme, the greatest of all Sacraments.

Thou hast within Thyself, in truth, all holiness. Ah, what am I saying! Thou art Holiness itself! Absolutely identical with God, Thou hidest beneath Thine inanimate veils the Holy of Holies, Jesus, Son of the Father, substantially Holy in His divine Person; holy in His soul through a created holiness which filled it from the first instant of His incarnation; holy also from an endless number of good and perfect works, works loaded with merit, fruits of repeated acts of heroic virtue, winning for Him a glorious crown of Holiness, Holiness which abides, ever undiminished, Holiness ever living, ever real.

Not satisfied art Thou, O Eucharistic Saviour, to have in Thyself, to be, this Holiness; Thou givest freely of Thy treasure. When my soul receives Thee, however unworthy Thou knowest it to be, Thou deliverest up to it the Holy with neither division nor diminution, without the slightest reserve. And then, graciously, in Thy transcendent love, Thou workest wonders within this soul, bringing about growths of grace, transformations more and more marvelous, all with but one object, one alone, to make this soul like unto God, sole type of all possible holiness, to assimilate it to this liv-

---

[1] St Thomas Aquinas, *Summa*, III, q. 60, a. 1.

ing image of holiness now presented to its view and so make it truly holy.

But, wondrous Sacrament, Thou art also the sign and symbol of holiness, sign and symbol of this operation of grace in my soul. Thou recordest in very truth its cause, its nature, its final goal.

First, its cause. That is Thy most blessed Passion, Lord Jesus: all, in Thy wondrous Sacrament, sings the glory of the Last Supper, of Thy Cross and Resurrection, of Thy reward. And all this imparts Thy holiness to me. Each time I receive Thy Sacrament, I see Thy love pass before me, I contemplate it and wonder, overcome by Thine "excess."[2]

Next, its nature. Thy Sacrament is a symbol of the nature, the essence, of this holiness; that is, the grace, the virtues, the gifts, the beatitudes, all the divine energies which the Spirit of Jesus, as Sacred Host, accumulates in the soul entirely possessed by Thy Sacrament of holiness.

Last, its final goal. Thou art a symbol, O Sacrament of the living, of eternal life, of confirmed holiness, of possession of our great God and Saviour Jesus Christ, Who is Himself this infinite, ever-during life.

This threefold relation with the past, present, and future is celebrated in that immortal anthem of the Church on Thy day of triumph, *Corpus Christi: O sacrum convivium*, sacred banquet, wherein Christ is received, the memory of His Passion is renewed, the soul is filled with grace, and the pledge of future glory is given to us....

Yes, all the Sacraments comprehend this threefold meaning, but none proclaims it as Thou proclaimest it, Holy Eucharist of God, when my soul is held in wonder before the rites which honor Thee, when it attempts to sound the depths of holiness Thou revealest therein....

Therefore art Thou called *a wonderful Sacrament*, an expression which Thy faithful people, in its language of faith, has translated: *the Most Holy Sacrament*, the Sacrament, that is, of perfect and highest holiness, the holiness of God Himself.

The Most Holy Sacrament! What penetrating sweetness is in this name! One feels one's soul seized with reverence when one simply pronounces it; indeed it is as if the mere utterance of it were enough to call up before our ravished eyes the adorable reality it contains.

The Most Holy Sacrament! Yes, of the seven Sacraments it is the most holy,

---

2 Luke 9: 31. Latin *excessus*, death. The author plays upon this word in its double meaning, Latin and modern (Translator).

because it is first in dignity, in sublimity, in power to make saints, because it is the one to which the others tend as to their end and consummation.³ For, while the others have only an instrumental virtue, a virtue given to them by Jesus Christ, Thou, O ineffable Sacrament, containest the Christ Himself, really, truly, and substantially, Thou, Author and very substance of grace....

O wondrous Sacrament, I adore Thee with my whole heart's devotion! I adore Thee, O God Who hidest Thyself beneath such fragile appearances! I adore Thee, and in contemplating Thee, losing myself in the immensity of Thy mystery, I am carried away, ravished in this faith which makes my entire being subject to Thee.... *Adoro te devote, latens Deitas.*⁴

---

3 St Thomas Aquinas.
4 Humbly I adore Thee, hidden Deity (Hymn of St Thomas).

XX

PASSIONIS TUAE MEMORIAM

A MEMORIAL OF THY PASSION

The wondrous Sacrament, the Most Holy of all Sacraments, was, in the thought of Jesus Christ, to be the eternal memorial of His "too great love," of His "excess of love," of that "excess"[1] He was to accomplish next day, when, His arms outstretched upon the Cross of Calvary as if in a sublime prayer, He would *offer Himself to God for a Sacrifice of sweetness.*[2]

Only shortly before, at the Last Supper, the same night in which He was betrayed, He had commanded—as the Apostle tells us: *This do for the commemoration of Me; eat of this Bread, drink of this Chalice in memory of Me,*[3] in memory of Jesus Christ, your Priest, your Victim, your Altar....

In memory of Me.... Lord, it is as if Thou saidst: "My little children, I have loved you too greatly, even beyond all bounds, *usque in finem dilexit;*[4] thus, of Myself, freely, I am going to be Your victim, *I Who have power to lay down My life without any man's being able to take it away from Me;*[5] and this Victim I Myself, as Priest, shall immolate upon the Altar of My sacred Humanity. My blood will flow—the Blood of God, *a great price*[6]—on this Most Holy Altar; it will save you, it will sanctify you, it will glorify you, it will be your Redemption....

"But you might forget My *excess;* man is ungrateful even for love, yes, even for the love of a God Who dies for him in extremest love, in an inconceivable depth of suffering....

"What shall I do that you may never more forget My *excess,* the death of Jesus Christ?...

"I bless this Bread. *Take ye, and eat; it is My Body which is given for you. Drink ye of this Chalice; it is My Blood which shall be shed for all unto remission*

---

1 Luke 9: 31. Latin *excessus* (Translator).
2 Eph. 5: 2.   3 1 Cor. 11: 24 *ff.*   4 He joined them unto the end (John 13: 1).
5 *Cf.* John 10: 17–18.   6 1 Cor. 6: 20.

of sins.[7[*... As often as you shall do this, you shall do it for the commemoration of Me, for you shall show the death of your Lord,*[8] Jesus Christ....

"Look you: just as tomorrow My Blood will be separated from My Body, so do I separate it here. Tomorrow the death of your Lord will take place; here, I represent it. Both one and the immolation, being voluntary, will offer to God an atonement of infinite merit, will carry off the victory, gain Heaven for you.... Then do this in memory of My blessed Passion, *tam beatae Passionis,*[9] yes, *in memory of Me....*

"With the extravagance of a loving God, I shall pay tomorrow the price of this redemption; and my *excess,* the overflowing bounty of my love, will call forth an answering love from you.... *Do this in memory of Me....*

"*In memory of Me,* in memory of My redeeming love, the sublime drama of which I begin here at this Last Supper and mean to perpetuate in the Holy Mass; *in memory of Me* Who institute the Sacrifice according to the rite of Melchisedech, a real Sacrifice, one with that of the Cross, and destined, in accordance with My adorable title of *perpetual Victim*, simply to be prolonged throughout the centuries, *until I come again* to take you to Myself in everlasting glory, the imperishable fruit of this same Sacrifice.

"*In memory of Me* and of this blessed Passion, into which are pressed and heaped the merits of My whole life; this blessed Passion, in which My life attains and perfects its fruitfulness; this blessed Passion, which tomorrow, more poignant than ever, will consecrate Me the universal Victim of sin-laden humanity, the Victim Whose ever-essential role, that is, to bestow upon souls the merits of the Redemption by Me accomplished, I shall perpetuate upon your altars for all time through the ministry of my priests...."

O Memorial of Jesus Christ, Memorial of His blessed Passion, I adore thee, I praise thee, I give thee thanks! Thou art the most sublime act of religion; thou art religion itself.... O Holy Mass, thou art the Eucharist, the Sacrifice and Sacrament of eternal life!

---

7 Luke 22: 19 and Matt. 26: 28. 8 *Cf.* 1 Cor. 11: 26.
9 Prayer *Unde et memores* of the Mass.

XXI

REDEMPTIONIS TUAE FRUCTUM

THE FRUIT OF THY REDEMPTION

Grant us, we beseech Thee, so to venerate the sacred mysteries of Thy Body and Blood that we may ever feel within us the fruit of Thy Redemption.

So does the Church, after stating the dogma of the Holy Eucharist, now indicate its spiritual value in our lives. Beautiful and profound prayer! How clearly it reveals, not only our duties in regard to these sublime mysteries, but also the special grace their observance confers upon us!

First our duties, my duties, in regard to the Holy Eucharist: *ita sacra mysteria venerari*.[1]... My worship must be complete. I must remember always, Lord Jesus, that Thy mysteries are two: Eucharistic Sacrifice and Eucharistic Sacrament, or, rather, a single adorable mystery under two aspects, which, illumining each other, enflame my heart with love.

Two mysteries, but what glorious unity! For, although distinct one from the other, they possess a perfect harmony, complete each other, and form a single mystery within the solemn rite which celebrates them, that is, the Holy Mass. There they are fused into one; there, more than anywhere else, I adore them.

True, I do worship Thee elsewhere: before the tabernacle I can lose myself in Thy presence, adore Thee, praise Thee, love Thee; when, in imposing processions, Thou passest as Ruler and King, I can follow Thee, Jesus, Sacred Host; in exultant song I can confess how absolute and how divine is Thy sway over peoples, and homes, and hearts. Yet never elsewhere as at Holy Mass can I worship Thee with that perfect adoration which is *the* Christian devotion to the Holy Eucharist both as Sacrifice and Sacrament. All else but fills up the measure; here I honor the very essence of Thine

---

[1] So to venerate the sacred mysteries.

entire worship, that worship in which I give myself up to God Thy Father as a victim with Thee, Who art Victim and eternal Priest of the Holy Eucharist, that worship by which I participate in these offices of Priest and Victim, to become one with Thee, infinite Love, and with my brothers, whom, through the Eucharist, I love especially.

Here, then, is the soul of my religion: to celebrate the Holy Mass in which I receive the Most Holy Sacrament, or, again, being present thereat, to receive Holy Communion, offering myself with Thee, Lord Jesus, as a sacrifice to God and incorporating myself with Thee, that I may abide in Thee and Thou in me!...

The soul of my worship is this: to take active part in Thine; that is, it is for me to stand every morning at the foot of this cross set up anew on the Calvary of thousands of altars; it is for me to be lifted up on it in oblation with Thee, in order to complete, so to speak, Thy perpetual sacrifice, Thine unceasing oblation, uniting my cross to Thine, seeing my suffering beside the agony borne by Thee; it is to accustom myself in this way, little by little—so slow is this lesson in the learning—and ever better and better, to conceive of my Christian life, my religious and priestly life, as an actual participation in Thy most blessed Passion, *tam beatae Passionis*—to so will it, to so live it...

This is the soul of my religion: at the Priest's Communion, at my own priestly Communion, to enter as it were into Thee, O my Christ so beloved! For so will this sacrificial action be more complete, more powerful, more divine. It is to be, as I participate in all Thine intentions as Victim, ever more truly inspired, ever more thoroughly imbued, with Thy spirit of self-abnegation, of forgetfulness of Thyself; it is to descend from Thine altar girded in the might of my God, whose Sacred Heart beats in my bosom, it is to go to my duty, to my suffering, to my victory over my passions; it is to die to myself, it is to live for Thee....

That is the Eucharistic worship which I desire to live; it is the Christian's devotion, my devotion, the supreme devotion, dominating, ruling, sustaining all others, lacking which these could only distort and destroy piety. He who lives this devotion plucks every moment from the Tree of Life which Thou art, O Jesus, the fruit of the Redemption. *Redemptionis tuae fructum*....

But what is this Fruit, this Fruit of Redemption but Thee? That I know and do believe: my Holy Mass is not only a Sacrifice of praise and thanksgiving, a simple memorial of that offered at the Last Supper and on Thy holy Cross; no, it is, besides, a true Sacrifice of propitiation which appeases Thy Father, our Father, my Father, and calls down His mercy upon us.[2] For Thou art truly the Victim in this act of propitiation!

I know and do believe, O Fruit of Redemption, that if I offer in sacrifice this Victim, this most holy Victim which Thou art, with a pure heart, a living faith, and a deep sorrow for my sins, I know and do believe that without fail I shall obtain mercy from this Father and the help of His grace in my need, in life, in death, in time, and for eternity.

I know and do believe, O Fruit of Redemption, that the fragrance exhaled by Thy Sacrifice is so pleasing to Him that He will accord unto me the gift of grace and repentance and the pardon of which I stand in such great need.

I know and do believe, O Fruit of Redemption, Lord Jesus, that Thy Sacrifice benefits not only me who offer it, who participate in it, but also all my brethren in Thee, those here on earth and those who are suffering in Purgatory, at the same time as it gives rejoicing and honor to those who dwell already in the glory of Heaven.

O Fruit of my Redemption, it is Thou, in short, Whom I seize upon in this Sacrifice, Whom I taste, Whose delights I savor; Thou, Lord Jesus, ever more truly known, more willingly obeyed, more devotedly served, ever more and more purely loved; Thou, preferred before all the world, before creatures, before myself; Thou, God of battles, Who establishest Thyself within my very heart and there meditatest combats and victories, making assault upon my passions....

Thou, O Jesus, art the Fruit of the Redemption, Thou Who conquerest within me the vehement desire for well-being, for ease and luxury, and all forms of pleasure, Who defeatest my greed of riches; yes, Thou, Who enchainest my ever-restless senses and preservest to them the virginal splendor of chaste hearts.

Thou, O Jesus, art the Fruit of the Redemption, Thou Who shatterest my vanity, my pride, Who tramplest on my truly silly self-worship, and subduest my soul to the peace of the poor in spirit. Yes, in a word, it is Thou, Lamb of God, Supreme Love, Goal of life, Who establishest within

---

2 *Catechism of the Holy Council of Trent*, CXX, 58.

me Thy heavenly kingdom, beginning it here below in the labors of exile, making Thy justice firm therein, stabilizing it, sanctifying it in the battle, to bring it to glorious completion above, in the splendor of Thy saints. It is a kind of gradual deification, almost a change of man into God, so that he can say: And I live, now not I; but Christ liveth in me.[3]

The Fruit of Thy Redemption, my God. Ah, let me eat of It constantly, *jugiter*, with desire unabated; not simply once a year, nor once a month, nor once a week, but every day, *jugiter*, O daily and supersubstantial Bread, Which art come down from Heaven, provided that Thy grace be with me and my soul seek Thee with an integrity that knows no deceit.

Courage, O my soul; thou desirest to conquer thyself, thou desirest to be victorious over thyself, in order to live, to live according to the exact measure by which thou wilt be able to die! Then eat of this Fruit, and thou wilt die never more; in thine inmost being, hearken to Him Who, assimilating thee to Himself, cries out to thee: *"Confidite, Ego vici mundum*—Have confidence, I have overcome the world."[4]

---

[3] Gal. 2: 20.   [4] John 16: 33.

XXII

PER DOMINUM NOSTRUM JESUM CHRISTUM

THROUGH JESUS CHRIST OUR LORD

Whenever the priest at the altar is about to utter the solemn formula of this supplication which is the end of his prayer, he rejoins his hands, which before had been outstretched in a gesture expressive of the lifting of his soul to his heavenly Father.

O Father, this special grace for which I cry out to Thee in the name of Thy Church, in the name of this people gathered here at Thy feet, sometimes, also, in my own name, this grace I implore *through our Lord Jesus Christ Thy Son, Who liveth and reigneth with Thee, in the unity of the Holy Ghost, world without end.*[1]

This Son of Thy dilection from eternity, the Well-beloved of all Thy complacent delight, Him I clasp again, so to speak, I take Him into my arms; I press Him to my priestly heart and, uniting myself to Him, ever heard, *ever graciously heard by Thee because of the honor Thou showest Him,*[2] I dare to approach the sublime throne of Thy Majesty; I dare to offer Him unto Thee as He is, with all that He is, all that He has, with all His perfections, His rights, and His merits, with the ever victorious power of His supreme mediation, in order that Thou mayest graciously hear Thy Church, all the souls here present as well as Thy priest, their unworthy representative. *Per Dominum nostrum.*[3]

So do I pray when, mounting the steps of the altar, I come to this table, image of the Holy of Holies; so do I entreat to be permeated with that purity of heart which is necessary for one who would minister in Thy sanctu-

---

1 This is not the formula of the *Deus qui nobis*, which ends: *Qui vivis et regnas cum Deo Patre,* Who liveth and reigneth with God the Father, etc., as it is addressed to our Saviour Himself (Translator's note).
2 Heb. 5: 7.   3 Through our Lord...

ary. Yes, through Jesus Christ Himself, *the Holy, the Innocent, the Undefiled, separated from sinners, and made higher than the Heavens,*[4] through Him I implore His own purity. *Per Christum Dominum nostrum.*[5]

So do I pray when, at the *Collect,* in which the desires of the faithful and the prayers of those present are summed up, I send up to the Father the cry of His Son interceding for us. *Per Dominum nostrum Jesum Christum.*[6]

So do I pray when, before announcing the Holy Gospel, I bow down, entreating Almighty God to cleanse my lips with the burning coal, *per Christum Dominum nostrum.*

So do I pray at the *Offertory,* when I pour into my chalice the little drop of water—symbol of the soul—which is lost in the wine that is to become the Most Precious Blood, Blood of the Word Which dwells in the Bosom of the Father, *Jesus Christus, Filius tuus, Dominus noster.*[7]

So do I pray when I bless the incense which is to give a sweet savor to the oblation of bread and wine and make it, in advance, through the intercession of St Michael, pleasing before the Face of this Father—the incense which is another symbol of the sweetness of Jesus Christ when, diffused over those present, it makes them sharers in the benediction assured to this oblation. *Per Christum Dominum nostrum.*

So do I pray when, bowing before the Holy Trinity of Father, Son, and Holy Spirit, at the *Suscipe, sancta Trinitas,*[8] I make the final offering of the Sacrifice of all the people, and of my own, too, *meum ac vestrum,*[9] in honor of God, of the Blessed Virgin Mary, and of all the saints, as well as for our own salvation. *Per Christum Dominum nostrum.*

So do I pray in the Secret of the Mass, when I place before God the *sacrifice of praise,* namely, this bread and this wine, as well as all the members of the Lord Jesus which they represent with Him, supplicating the Lord to make thereof an acceptable offering. *Per Dominum nostrum Jesum Christum.*

So do I pray ever more solemnly, when, at the *Preface to the Eucharistic Action,* lifting my hands toward the heights of God and reciting one after the other the mysteries of our holy religion, I give praise to Him Who did enact them, Who still enacts them, bearing clear to the throne of His Father

---

[4] Heb. 7: 26.
[5] Through Christ our Lord.
[6] Through our Lord Jesus Christ.
[7] Jesus Christ, Thy Son, our Lord.
[8] Receive, O Holy Trinity.
[9] Ut meum ac vestrum sacrificium … That my sacrifice and yours…

the seraphic exultation of the adoring angels, their eternal and threefold *Sanctus. Per Christum Dominum nostrum.*

So do I pray at the most holy Prayer of the *Canon*, the changeless rite of the *Consecration*, when, my eyes raised to Heaven towards the most merciful Father, I pray and beseech Him to vouchsafe to receive and bless the gifts, the offerings, the holy sacrifice which we offer Him for the Church, for her Head, for our Bishop, for the King,[10] for all those united in the same faith, the same love. *Per Jesum Christum Filium tuum Dominum nostrum.*[11]

So do I pray, in the flight which bears me and all present toward God, when I call to my aid the Blessed Virgin Mary and the Apostles and Martyrs of Jesus. *Per eumdem Christum Dominum nostrum.*[12]

So do I pray when I stretch out my hands over the offering as over the Head of the perpetual Victim, Who reigns in Heaven, in the Bosom of the Father and at His right Hand, Who is about to descend to earth again to renew His mystery here, and Whose sublimity imposes upon me a momentary silence, that I may adore Him Who is my entire Prayer. *Per Christum Dominum nostrum.*

He has come down into my hands.... He is here, on the altar, for me, for all, here before His Father, before ravished Heaven and earth.... He is verily all Prayer, the sole *Victim, pure, holy, and immaculate:* the *Holy Sacrifice* Which attracts God's peaceful and merciful regard; He is the eternal Lamb of Offering, Which He Himself, Angel of the Father, bears—yes, for this I implore Him, prostrate in spirit—clear to the sublime Altar on high, into the glory of Heaven, even to the Altar of His holy and victorious Humanity, into the greater Temple of the Bosom of His Father, there to become an ever more ardent supplication, a source of ever richer graces. *Per eumdem Christum Dominum nostrum.*

Through Him is graciously heard the *Memento* of those who have gone to sleep in Him, to enter into the place of refreshment and peace; through Him the prayer of the Church Militant rises to the God of mercy, interceding for sinners in this world. *Per Christum Dominum nostrum.*

Through Him, and *with Him*, and *in Him*, in the majestic echo of the final *Amen* of this sublime prayer, is presented to the Father, in the unity of the Holy Ghost, the most pure *Oblation* which He became, to the praise

---

10 In Belgium. 11 Through Jesus Christ Thy Son our Lord.
12 Through the same Christ our Lord.

of Almighty God and His eternal glory. *Per Ipsum, et cum Ipso, et in Ipso.*[13]

It is our Lord Jesus Christ Himself Who sings His own Prayer, the *Pater noster,* in which He begins to entreat our participation—by means of the Communion now so very near—in the Sacrifice He has just offered; with this end in view, also, He prays for our liberation from all evil and invokes that sweet union of peace with God and our Brethren at the Breaking of the Bread over the Precious Blood—with which He would fain inebriate us. *Per eumdem Dominum nostrum Jesum Christum.*[14]

So shall I pray when, filled with His Body, yes, inebriated with this Blood which springs forth the virgin souls of priests,[15] I voice at the Postcommunion the prayer of the entire Church to obtain the full fruit of His Sacrifice. *Per Dominum nostrum Jesum Christum.*

And now God has a last blessing for me, the one which confirms the propitiatory power of this Sacrifice, *for me and for all those for whom I have offered it.* Again and always it is through Jesus Christ that the Heavenly Father grants this blessing. *Per Christum Dominum nostrum. Amen.*

I trust myself then in everything to Thee, to Thee alone, O my Priest and my Sacrifice, supreme Mediator between God and man. It is meet that I do so; it is just, right, and availing unto salvation. Only that is prayer which passes through Thy mediation.

O Father of our Lord Jesus Christ, Father of Him Who is *ours* by every title; Father of Jesus, our Saviour; Father of our Christ, our Priest! Have pity on us for His sake, by reason of His wounds every crying out to Thee and ever compassionately heard!

He lives with Thee, *qui tecum vivit,*[16] possessing the Life which Thou art and which He desires to be for us. He reigns with Thee, *et regnat,*[17] over the Church, the heritage won by His victory; He lives and reigns with Thee, indissolubly united to Thee by the substantial chain of Love, in the unity of the Holy Spirit, of Thine own substance, united to Thee, the God Whom I adore and before Whose Face all creatures acknowledge their nothingness—*in unitate Spiritus Sancti, Deus.*[18]

So has it been from all eternity and so will it be forever, world with-

---

13 Through Him, and with Him, and in Him.
14 Through the same Jesus Christ Our Lord.
15 Zac. 9: 17.   16 Who liveth with Thee.   17 And reigneth ...
18 In the unity of the Holy Ghost, one God.

out end. O let it be so always for the consolation of those whom, through Jesus Christ our Lord, Thou ever mercifully hearest. *Per omnia saecula saeculorum.*[19]

Amen. So be it; it is well so. I believe, I adore, and I abandon myself to His love. *Amen.*

---

19 For ever and ever.

XXIII

DONEC VENIAT

UNTIL HE COME[1]

When shalt Thou come again, Lord Jesus? Beneath impenetrable veils Thou appearest today to my adoring gaze; when, oh, when shalt Thou burst upon my sight in Thy glory, in that radiant light which Thou art, wherein I shall be lost before the vision of Thy Face, which *shineth as the sun in his power?*[2] *Donec veniat.*

Donec veniat.... Until Thou come again! *Donec....* How heavy with tears is this word, how fraught with impatience, with longing and hope! *Donec...* until ... Ah, that looking forward to Thy coming, to the day when Thou shalt descend to us, borne on the clouds, with heralding angels, Thy triumphant host outspread in incomparable, divine array! When Thou shalt come down to us and we shall arise to come at last to Thee, Lord, O Only and Well-beloved! When Thou shalt come down even to me who kneel before Thy Sacred Host, repeating to myself, *donec veniat....*

Donec veniat! Until Thou come again to me, who have believed, who shall see Thee and be taken up to meet Thee, to meet my Christ, with all those who have believed, who shall see ... *nos simul rapiemur in nubibus obviam Christo in aera.*[3]

Donec veniat. Until Thou come to judge the living and the dead, those who are to live forever, those who are to die forever, the former for having believed in Thee, O Jesus-Eucharist, the latter for having refused to believe in Thee, *Spes unica mundi;*[4] only hope of this world!... Until Thy kingdom come which *shall have no end.*[5] *Donec aera.*[6]

So shall I watch, Lord Jesus, and look forward to Thy coming; and to

---

1 Epistle of *Corpus Christi*.   2 Apoc. 1: 16.
3 We shall be taken up in the clouds to meet Christ into the air (1 Thes. 4: 16).
4 Prayer of Holy Saturday.   5 *Credo.*
6 We shall be taken up in the clouds to meet Christ into the air (1 Thes. 4: 16).

comfort myself throughout this long, all too long waiting, I shall make oblation of Thee, I shall taste Thy sweetness, Holy Eucharist; *I shall announce the death of the Lord* each time I do this; I shall live by the memory of His death, of His resurrection, of His glorious ascension; by the sublime mystery of life which overcame death,[7] *in mei memoriam;*[8] and I shall take courage, whilst, penetrating Thy veils with the eyes of my faith, I shall adore Thee humbly, hidden Deity, my spirit failing with love before Thine altars.[9]

Ego enim accepi.[10] That is what Thou Thyself hast taught me; that is what Thy great apostle cries out to me: *donec veniat* ... until Thou come again, until this exile cease at last, the exile in this valley of tears, *in hac lacrymarum valle.*

Come, Lord Jesus, come! *Veni, Domine Jesu!*[11] This is the last word of Holy Scripture. May it be the very breath of my priestly and Christian life! *Veni, veni, Domine Jesu!*

As the hart panteth after the fountains of water; so my soul panteth after Thee.[12] I long for the fountains of Thy glorious wounds, O Jesus; I thirst for the living waters of grace and holiness which break forth therefrom in torrents, *de fontibus Salvatoris.*[13] These fountains are here in Thy Sacred Host, and I, *in a desert land, and where there is no way, and no water* ... *in terra deserta, et invia, et inaquosa,*[14] long to still my thirst thereat....

I thirst for Thee, O Jesus Christ, for Thee, the living God! My tears are my bread day and night,[15] so soon as I revive Thy memory, so soon as my eyes, raised to Thy Sacred Host, the Divine Victim, glimpse dimly my Father's house. *Sitivit in te anima mea, haec recordatus sum usque ad domum Dei.*[16]

Quare tristis es, anima mea?[17] Be not sorrowful, O my soul; be no longer sorrowful! What more desirest thou in Heaven than already thou hast on earth, when, before the holy altar, thou contemplatest the Sacred Host, forgetting all else in adoration of the *Salvation of thy countenance:* when, as Thy prayer becomes more fervent, thou enterest into—almost thou art

7 *Cf. Preface* of Easter.
8 In memory of Me.
9 *Adoro te.*
10 For I have received....
11 Come, Lord Jesus (Apoc. 22: 20).
12 Ps. 41.
13 Out of the Saviour's fountains (Isa. 12: 3)
14 Ps. 62: 3.
15 Ps. 41: 4.
16 For Thee my soul hath thirsted. These things I remembered, even to the house of God (Ps. 62: 2 and Ps. 41: 5).
17 Why art Thou sad, O my soul?

transformed into—thy God, thy life. *Spera.... Salutare vultus mei.... Apud me oratio Deo vitae meae!* [18]

Donec veniat. I shall await, O Lord, Thy coming. Until then I will be victim with Thee, priest with Thee. Until then I *will bear* in my soul *the marks of Thy death,* [19] O Jesus, and live on the altar with Thee.

Donec veniat.... Come, oh, come, and delay no longer! I cry out to Thee with the singer of Thy Eucharistic hymn: I implore Thee, *Oro, fiat illud, quod tam sitio,* grant me at last that for which my soul so thirsteth; grant me one day to see Thee unveiled; let me be a happy witness of Thy glory, ravished in Thine own felicity ... *visu sim beatus tuae gloriae!* [20]

---

18 With me is prayer to the God of my life.   19 Gal. 6: 17.   20 *Adoro te.*

XXIV

PROBET SEIPSUM HOMO[1]

LET A MAN PROVE HIMSELF

Before such sublime Mysteries, before the Body and Blood of the Lord, my soul is overtaken with fear.... But then! Even the heavenly Powers adore them trembling,[2] and wherefore should I not be seized with awe in the presence of the Godhead, I, in my nothingness?...

Am I pure enough to approach Thee thus, O my God, so lightly, so familiarly, and every day, too; Thee, Who perceivest the most secret blemishes, even in Thine Angels; Thee, *the searcher of hearts and reins,*[3] before Whom the most humiliating faults of every creature lie revealed? O Jesus Christ, Thou Purity of Virgins, how regardest Thou Thy creature when, each morning, burdened with his own nature, he approaches Thy holy altar and takes Thee into his weak and wretched creature hands, capable therefore of all evil? *Probet seipsum homo.*

I know, Lord Jesus, that Thy Church exacts of me as preparation only a right intention in the state of grace; that I know. I know that Thy Holy Eucharist is not a reward, but a remedy; that consequently It is for the sick, both in body and soul; that one comes to It to be made clean, to be made more and more pure, to be freed insensibly from venial sin, aye, even from all imperfections; that It is the antidote for the deadly sin which would destroy my soul. I know all this, and yet—?

Probet autem seipsum homo. Let a man prove himself, the Apostle admonishes me. To receive unworthily, that is, not in Thy grace, to eat the Bread Which Thou art, to drink Thy Precious Blood, unworthily, would be, he says, a frightful thing. Since the Holy Eucharist is the Memorial of Thy Passion, since It represents and re-enacts that Passion on our altars, to eat or to drink thereof unworthily, without the love of God in our hearts,

---

[1] Epistle of *Corpus Christi.*   [2] *Preface* of the Mass.   [3] Ps. 7: 10.

would be to renew the crimes which caused Thy suffering, from Judas' sacrilegious kiss, to the insults offered Thee on Calvary.

To receive Thy Holy Eucharist thus, O Jesus Christ, would make me guilty of an appalling sacrilege, the profanation of Thy Body and Thy Blood, *reus erit Corporis et Sanguinis Domini:*[4] and then, as just punishment, I should be eating and drinking my own eternal damnation, *judicium sibi manducat et bibit.*[5] Ah! Let me rather be guilty of any other crime, of all crimes but that; oh, never, never of that one! *Probet seipsum homo.*

Then prove thyself, O my soul; and each morning when thou preparest thyself for the Sacrifice of the Lord, make examination of thyself. Lest the eye of God pierce thee through and through, judging thee, enter thou into judgment with thyself. Shake off thy dust, thou, born of God; clothe thyself in innocence, in love, in perfect confidence. Seek out thy God with singleness of heart.

Let Him be thy wedding garment shining white, without which thou shalt in no wise be admitted to the Bridegroom's feast. This robe is woven by charity, by divine love, that fire of God which cleanses from every stain and bears Thee upward to the tender embrace, the encircling arms of the Best-beloved.

Lord Jesus, Purity of Angels, clothe me in Thyself, that I may come to The, not with any honor of my own, for I have none, but with Thine own, which is very holiness. Do Thou array me Thyself for my coming to Thee each morning, for my tryst with Thee in the midst of Thine angels, who attend Thee at Thy holy altar.

---

4 He shall be guilty of the body and of the blood of the Lord (1 Cor. 11: 27).
5 He eateth and drinketh judgment to himself.

XXV

ANIMOSA FIRMAT FIDES[1]

DAUNTLESS FAITH ATTESTS

I adore Thee, Holy Eucharist, *Mystery of faith,*[2] mystery in which I adore by faith what I comprehend not, nor see, what is beyond the order of nature, *praeter rerum ordinem,* but not beyond Thine infinite power, O Jesus Christ, Bread of God! This Bread is Thy Flesh; this Wine is Thy Blood. *Credo, Domine.*

I adore Thee in all faith, O Jesus Christ, Mystery of God, wholly present under each species, that of the Bread, that of the Wine; I adore Thee, O Flesh divine, food of the soul, O Blood divine, fountain of Life eternal! Receiving the one, receiving the other, I possess my God whole and entire....

I adore Thee with all my faith, O Jesus Christ, Thee Whom I shall receive unbroken, undivided, entire, in the fullness of Thy power, perfect God, perfect Man!

My faith adores Thee, O Jesus Christ, Thee Whom one or a thousand will receive, yet Whom one will receive in Thy totality, whole and entire, as will a thousand others, and Whom all will consume without ever exhausting Thee.

My faith adores Thee, O Jesus Christ, Thee, Whom both the good and the wicked receive—yet with what opposite results! For in Thee the former find life, but the latter their own condemnation; the same food to both, Thou producest, nevertheless, quite different effects, according as Thy love penetrates or not into the inmost chamber of the soul.

My faith adores Thee, O Jesus Christ, Who in Thine indivisible substance, art present in the smallest fragment as perfectly as in the Sacred Host entire. Though the simple form, the appearance, be broken, nothing is diminished of the content, the Reality, either in its nature or grandeur.

---

1 *Sequence, Lauda Sion.*   2 *Consecration.*

Mystery of faith, I adore Thee, making known Thy glory so far as is in me; for infinitely Thou exceedest my praise, *nec laudare sufficis*.[3]

Would that I might make my priestly and Christian life a sacrifice of praise unto Thy Holy Eucharist, O Jesus Christ! Would that it might become a song of thanksgiving, the music of which should resound undying: a Eucharist unto the Holy Eucharist!

In the contemplation and adoration of this ineffable mystery, may my Christian faith seek, and find, and come to possess that vital force which will move it to attempt for Thee all that is great, noble, and generous in the exercise of my Christian life.

For in this plenitude of faith, in this faith ever more ardent, *animosa*, in this living faith in the Holy Eucharist, I should penetrate more and more deeply the total Mystery of the Incarnate Word; I should enter into Jesus Christ by the *door*[4] of His sacred Humanity, and so into possession of the promised *pastures*[5] where the Word is Himself the sustenance of His sheep.

Finally, my heart *purified by faith*,[6] by this faith in the Holy Eucharist, I should be enabled to lay hold more firmly on my God, to sense Him, to taste His sweetness, to be more and more clearly conscious of my divine adoption, to become more simply the child of the Father, to feel myself more strongly engrafted on the Christ Jesus, to abandon myself entirely to the influence of the Holy Spirit.... Yes, in such faith I should go more surely from the Holy Eucharist to the Blessed Trinity and should be more completely restored to the keeping of the Thrice-Holy God from Whom I came, unto Whom I return. I believe, Lord; do Thou increase my faith! *Nil hoc verbo veritatis verius*.[7]

---

[3] From *Lauda Sion: Quia major omni laude nec laudare sufficis*—Because He is above all praise, thou dost not suffice to praise Him.
[4] John 10: 9.   [5] *Ibid*.   [6] Acts 15: 9.
[7] Nothing can be truer than Truth's very Word (*Adoro te*).

XXVI

CARO MEA, CIBUS, SANGUIS MEUS, POTUS[1]

MY FLESH IS MEAT INDEED, AND MY BLOOD IS DRINK INDEED

Ah, what solace in these words! Their truth I accept, I adore; I make in them an act of faith: yes, Lord Jesus Christ, I believe with all my soul that Thy Holy Eucharist is indeed my meat, is in very truth my drink; I believe Thou didst institute It, that I should hunger never again, nor thirst, that all earthly delight should fade in my sight, and that I should cleave to Thee alone, to Thee, Infinite Beauty, Supreme Love, Center of life! I so believe.

Both by Thy nature and Thy purpose, O wondrous Sacrament, Thou art a food, the celestial food of souls, of my soul. Body and Blood of Jesus Christ, life immortal of mortals, Thine it is to nourish them, to refresh them, to quench their thirst.

Nevertheless, in nourishing me thus, Thou wilt by no means be transformed into me, O Holy Eucharist of God; instead Thou wilt remake me in the image and semblance of my Saviour. His spirit, His life will invade my soul; my inmost being will become like unto Him and therefore almost divine. His love increasing in me, that love which is kindled today by this Holy Communion and made into a glowing fire, will work this transformation—His love, which is the particular and most excellent fruit of this wondrous Sacrament.

Bread of Pilgrims,[2] Thou art the sustenance of my spiritual life in my long quest for the fatherland of Heaven; Thou keepest my soul from growing faint, guardest it from all disaster, for Thou art the defense against sin and its destructive powers. Thou becomest the strength of my weakness; and

---

1 *Gospel* of Corpus Christi.   2 *Lauda Sion.*

if there be in me any generosity, I owe it to Thee, O Holy Sacrament, to Thee Who makest the martyrs of Jesus. *Sustentat*.[3]

Bread of Angels, no limit is set to my growth in God; I can progress constantly in grace before God and man; Thyself Thou givest increase of this grace in my soul, causest it to advance from virtue to virtue, and makest to shine in it ever more gloriously the light of the heavenly kingdom. *Auget*.[4]

O Bread of Heaven, Thou repairest our souls. Whoever receives Thee loses at last his indifference; Thou renewest in him the zeal of the saints; Thou repairest the losses in his spiritual organism resulting from his venial sins, his infidelities, from the imperfections of his fallen nature, constantly prone to all sin. Thou healest, Thou removest every obstacle in the way of the activity of God in his soul. Thou art the strength of Jesus Christ therein. *Reparat*.[5]

O Holy Eucharist, Bread of the saints, Thou art the soul's joy, sublime and chaste; Thou art its fathomless consolation; Thou are its sole, its unspeakable delight. Through Thee it experiences the transports, the raptures, the ecstacies of love; all its intoxication of joy comes from having partaken of Thee, Body and Blood of Christ. Thou hast all that is delicious and the sweetness of every taste.[6] O Sweetness, O Fragrance, O Fullness of Joy! Happy they who hunger and thirst for Thee! Wheat of the elect, Thou bringest to man the reign of peace; Wine that inebriates, Thou springest forth virgins.[7] *Delectat*.[8]

But more! In transforming our souls, Thou changest by the power of Thy holy love even our bodies of clay. For in truth, when I enter into union with Thee, Thou invadest my whole being, my soul and its powers, my body, and its members. Sublime healer art Thou of soul and body, *reparatio mentis et corporis*,[9] this body and this soul, bought by Thee for a price, both worthy to share the healing power of Thy eucharistic grace, Thy work of Redemption.

To be sure, it is but indirectly and in secondary degree that my body undergoes this celestial eucharistic influence; but it does undergo it. Thy graces, O Jesus, Sacred Host, flow back from soul to body; Thou dispersest, divine Power of the altar, the force of the passions which might destroy my

---

3 It sustains (St Thomas).   4 It gives increase (*Ibid*).   5 It restores (*Ibid*).
6 Wis. 16: 20.   7 Zac. 9: 17.   8 It delights (St Thomas).
9 A renewal of mind and body (*Postcommunion* of Eighth Sunday after Pentecost).

soul; Thou makest of my members *instruments of justice unto God*.[10]

Eating Thy Flesh, drinking Thy Blood, O Lord, I receive substantially within myself Thine own Body, entering into ineffable union with it. Glorified Body of Jesus, each time Thou comest to me, Thou consecratest, so to speak, my sinful flesh, giving it in Thyself all dignity, all nobility; it enters into a kind of affinity with Thy holy Humanity, O Jesus; Thou incorporatest it with its divine Head, and behold, we are become almost "concorporate,"[11] *membra sumus corporis ejus, de carne ejus, de ossibus ejus.*[12] In a manner of speaking, Thou lookest upon my body as Thine own Body, Thou art heedful of it, that it may be made ever more like to the Body of Thy glory, *qui reformabit corpus humilitatis nostrae.*[13]

Ah, yes, *Thy Flesh is meat indeed, Thy Blood is drink indeed....* I believe this truth, Lord, I have proved it, I rejoice in it, and this it is that makes me forsake all the illusory joys of earth.

---

10 Rom. 6: 12–14.   11 St Cyril of Jerusalem.
12 We are members of His body, of His flesh, and of His bones (Eph. 5: 30).
13 Who will reform the body of our lowness (Phil. 3: 21).

XXVII

IN ME MANET ET EGO IN ILLO[1]

HE ABIDETH IN ME, AND I IN HIM

The eyes of all are turned towards Thee, O Lamb of God, Bread of Angels and men! All creatures hope in Thee, *Who givest them meat in due season. Thou openest Thy Hand and fillest every living creature with Thy blessing. Oculi omnium in te sperant, et tu das illis escam.*[2]

In this hour of the Holy Sacrifice, I, too, fix the gaze of my soul upon Thee in complete faith and hope and love, in expectation of Thy divine banquet; yes, I beg my sustenance of Thee, O Jesus, I beg Thy Flesh and Thy Blood, in order that Thou abide in me, and I in Thee. For I hunger and thirst for this union, this communion. *I in Thee, Thou in me!* Is this not the most sweet fruit of Thy Holy Eucharist?

"O Sacrament of loving-kindness! O Sign of oneness! O Bond of love!"[3]

I in Thee and Thou in me.... Love, love, and, again, love! That is the whole mystery; why seek further! Thou desirest that we love each other, Lord, and Thine incomparable love has devised this most wonderful secret: *I in Thee and Thou in me!* It suffices that I eat Thy Flesh and drink Thy Blood, and, behold, I am one with Thee, somewhat as Thou art One with Thy Heavenly Father; was not that Thine own prayer in the hour of Thy blessed Passion?[4]

Then come, Lord Jesus, come! Thou Who wilt be my Vine,[5] Whose desire is to make me Thy branch, come, implant Thyself deep in my soul, take root there; and then, Vine of the Father, let Thy divine sap rise, let

---

1 *Gospel* of Corpus Christi.
2 The eyes of all hope in Thee, O Lord: and Thou givest them meat (*Gradual* of Corpus Christi).
3 *O sacramentum pietatis! O signum unitatis! O vinculum caritatis!* (St Augustine, *In Joan.*, tract. 26, no. 13).
4 John 17: 21.   5 John 15.

it flow seething upward to give strong growth to the humble shoot which wishes to be in Thee, that Thou be also in it.

With what great tenderness, with what insistency Thou entreatest me: *Manete in me et ego in vobis!*[6] One would say it is Thou Who beggest love—Thou, of me, the beggar of God!

If I abide in Thee, what rich fruit my labors will bear! I am Thy consecrated priest, and even though I were not, it is still true that I can do nothing without Thee. But if I remain in Thee, if I never leave Thee, never tear myself from Thine embrace, ah, what power will be given to me! I shall come near to souls; and they, sensing Thy presence within me, will approach, will ask for themselves, too, the Bread of Life, in order that Thou be in them, and they in Thee. What truer apostolate?

Moreover, if I abide in Thee, Lord Jesus, if Thou abide in me, what power will be in my prayer! Thou givest me Thy promise: *You shall ask whatever you will, and it shall be done unto you.*[7]

Soon, now, Thou wilt come to me, my Saviour—to me so unworthy! Oh, let me, in that moment, be clearly conscious that Thou art in me and I in Thee! Yet, if it be not Thy will that I actually feel this union of my soul with God, how should it matter? Give me, nevertheless, to believe in Thee, Lord Jesus, to believe that Thy strength is welling up into the little branch, in order that it may live and breathe only by Thee, aspiring to God by Thine own aspiration. Yes, let me believe more and more firmly that Thy Life is my life, that mine has disappeared in Thee, *that I live, now not I, but Christ liveth in me.*[8]

I in Thee, Thou in me, to the end that we may be consummated and perfected in Oneness, *consummati in Unum.*[9]

---

6 Abide in Me, and I in you (John 15: 4).
7 John 15: 7.   8 Gal. 2: 20.   9 John 17: 23.

XXVIII

VIVET PROPTER ME[1]

HE SHALL LIVE BY ME

I in Thee, and Thou in me: that is perfect intercourse, mutual compenetration, true communion; it is the union, or a fusion, one might say, of God and man; Thou comparest it, Lord, to an *incorporation*, a mysterious *consanguinity* consummated between Thee and me. Ah, stay then, my Saviour! Let us remain in this oneness, I in Thee, Thou in me, that I may ever live by Thee! *Propter te, Domine!*

I who shall soon eat the Flesh of the Son of God I who shall drink of the chalice of His Precious Blood, I shall live by Jesus Christ, as He lives by His Father.... What is Thy meaning?

Just as there flows into Thee, O Jesus, the divine *torrent of pleasure*[2] descending from the Father; just as there blossoms forth plenteously in Thee the life of this Father Who begets Thee ineffably, indefatigably, eternally; so, while I abide in Thee, and Thou in me, I also am in some sort generated by Thee and proceed from Thee; Thou impartest to me this life of God, of Thy Father and mine, this superabundance of life, overflowing from Thee in sanctifying grace, in actual graces, in gifts of Thy Holy Spirit, in virtue upon virtue; freely Thou givest me life, Thy Life, and Thy desire is to give it me in *great abundance.*[3]

I live by Thee, most dear Lord, only Love of my soul; I live and breathe by Thee. Let the world forget me, know me not: my only desire henceforth is to be another Christ; living by Him, with Him, in Him, and, in that oneness effected in Jesus and myself by the Holy Spirit, giving to our Heavenly Father all honor and glory.

I live by Thee, my Christ, which is to say that, as I am nourished by Thee, so, from now on, I will no longer think but by Thee, by Thee love

---

1 *Gospel* of Corpus Christi.   2 Ps. 35: 9.   3 John 10: 10.

and pray and sing, by Thee suffer and labor and fight, by Thee die and gain the palm of victory.

I live by Thee, Eucharist of my God! Be Thou the soul of my soul, be all to me, All to my nothingness! Let me lose myself to find myself again in Thee, *not having my justice,* the fruit of my purely human activity, but *that which is of God, justice in faith,*[4] proceeding from my complete union with Thee, Lord, by Whom I would live, by Whom I would die.

Yes, by Whom I would die! O blessed death which gives me possession, active and real of such a life, of the life of Christ Jesus in me! Whoever loses his life shall find it in the Life eternal Which Thou art,[5] *Thou the true God and life eternal.*[6]

Our fathers did eat manna in the desert and are dead.[7] This manna was but a figure of the earthly nourishment which must pass and come to nothing. But Thou, O Jesus, are *the Bread by Which he who eateth shall live forever.*[8] Gone are all symbols, and I am in possession of the ineffable reality which Thou art: Thou livest, and I, if I eat of the Bread which gives life to the world[9] shall not die, but live forever.

O Life Which art Jesus Christ, I adore Thee! I subject my reason to the faith which reveres Thee, my heart to the love which embraces Thee. O divine Life, flow into my being, that my life may flow into Thine, that I may live henceforth only by Thee! What praise shall be to the Heavenly Father, when He shall see me thus only in His Son Jesus Christ!

---

4 Phil. 3: 9.
5 *Cf.* John 12: 25.
6 1 John 5: 20.
7 *Gospel* of Corpus Christi.
8 *Ibid.*
9 John 6: 33.

XXIX

CREDO

I BELIEVE

I believe in one God, the Father Almighty; I believe in one Lord Jesus Christ, the only-begotten Son of God, Who became Man, was crucified for us, and rose again from the dead; I believe in the Holy Ghost, the Lord and giver of life, Who together with the Father and the Son is adored and glorified; I believe in one holy Catholic and apostolic Church; I confess one Baptism; and I await the life everlasting. Amen.

Such is my profession of faith: the Holy Eucharist, *Mystery of faith*, is the Sacrament which maintains and vivifies it, which stills the thirst of my soul with the flood of life divine, the life revealed to me by the heavenly light of this faith.

O Father in Heaven, Thou hast had from all eternity a thought of me, Thine own sublime and profound thought, a thought comprehensive of my vocation both in time and in eternity, a thought ruled by Thy grace, a thought which at Thy good pleasure Thou wilt crown in heavenly glory: Thou wilt have me to be another Jesus, that *I may be found in Him, et inveniar in illo*,[1] and this in order that I become and remain Thy child, serving Thy praise forever and ever.[2] Thy thought, behold—is Jesus! I believe and I adore.

Son of God, Light of Light, consubstantial with the Father, I must cleave to Thee according to the degree of my vocation, to Thee, the Word Incarnate, Which I must body forth anew if I would remain in the thought of this Father, if I would realize it, live it. I must become another Christ, in order that this Father look upon me as His child. I believe and I adore.

O Holy Spirit of the Father and of the Son, it is by Thine interior influence that I shall be able to enter into this thought of the Father concerning

---

1 Phil. 3: 9. 2 Eph. 1: 5 and 6.

me, to transform myself into Jesus Christ, sharing His divinity according to His holy will. It is Thou Who wilt make me like unto the Lord Jesus, wilt reveal Him to me and accomplish within me the Thought of the Father. Yes, Thou, Holy Spirit, wilt unite me thus with my God, the Trinity I adore, wilt let my heart share in that intercourse of ineffable love, so that I shall cry out to this God, through Thee, Spirit of Jesus: "Father, Father!" And through Thee, Love of the Father and of the Son, I shall myself become love, wholly love! I believe and I adore.

I believe in Thy holy Church, my Mother, sublime minister of the redemption, prolongation of the life of Christ, *His Body, which He loved, for Which He delivered Himself up, that He might present it to Himself a glorious Church, not having spot or wrinkle, holy and without blemish.*[3] I am a member of this Body; I share in its splendid unity, its incomparable beauty; I am of the fellowship of His saints, I descend from His Apostles, I am the brother of all who are His. I believe and I rejoice unto the Lord.

By my holy Baptism, Thou didst engraft me on Thyself, O Jesus Christ; I entered thereupon into Thy sacred unity; all that is Thine forthwith became mine: Thy mysteries, Thy gifts, Thy graces. Vine of the saints, Thou madest me a humble branch, drawing its life thenceforth from Thee. Only the power of sin could tear me from Thy divine stock. What fertility is in this graft of God's saints! I believe and I thank Thee.

I believe in the Life eternal Which Thou art, Lord, and I await it; yes, unweariedly I fix my gaze on that supernal reality which alone upholds my courage in the exile in this valley of tears. *Et expecto,* I expect, I wait in hope; when shalt Thou come, Lord Jesus? Oh, quickly come! *Veni, Domine Jesu!*[4] This expectation is the only possible attitude for a priest, for a Christian.

But what is the force that lifts my spiritual powers to these heights of faith? What is the food which sustains them, renews them, increases them, transporting my being with unspeakable delights? Ah, what but Thy Holy Eucharist, mystery and epitome, from its inception, of this same faith! For does not this Eucharist contain Jesus Christ whole and entire? And through It do I not enter into God's eternal Thought of me, that mystery of predestination, redemption, sanctification, and salvation? Am I not entirely united with that Thought when I receive Thy Sacred Body, Thy Most Precious

---

3 Eph. 5: 27.   4 Apoc. 22: 20.

Blood, O my Jesus? Does not the Blessed Trinity, Father, Son, and Holy Spirit, dwell within me then just to make that Thought mine, to quicken my soul by its power, and help me to live by it?

Is it not the Holy Eucharist, Which, by uniting me with God, gives me communion with all the Church, so that I share in her unity, her sanctity, her apostolicity, her catholicity? Am I not consecrated by the power of this Eucharist in the Body of which Baptism made me a member?

Is it not the Holy Eucharist, *pledge of future glory,* Which implants in my soul, yea, even in my body, that leaven of immortality which will raise me up from death into the eternal rejoicing of the saints of Jesus? *Et expecto.*

My God, I believe; more firmly than ever do I believe in this Mystery of faith which guards and exalts my entire faith. Prostrate before Thee, I bless Thee, Light of the faithful, hidden Splendor Which is to burst forth into the glory of eternal Love. *Amen.*

UNION OF THE WILL

Suscipe

THE UNION OF THE WILL IS THE GOAL REACHED BY THE SOUL AS IT MOUNTS THE LADDER OF THE MASS, WHICH, BY THE HOLY EUCHARIST, BRINGS IT HOME TO GOD ITS FATHER. IN THIS UNION OF THE WILL THE SOUL EXPERIENCES A THREEFOLD MYSTERY: DETACHMENT, DEATH TO SELF, AND COMMUNION. THE MATTER IS SANCTIFIED, SEPARATED FROM PROFANE USES; IT BECOMES A VICTIM, CONSECRATED, OFFERED; AND IT IS GIVEN BY GOD IN COMMUNION TO THE SOUL. THUS LOVE FULFILLS THIS LABOR OF THE INMOST BEING WHICH TRANSFORMS IN GOD; THIS IS ACCOMPLISHED FROM THE OFFERTORY TO THE END OF THE MASS.

BENEDICTION OF THE MATTER

From the Offertory to the Preface

IN ORDER TO BECOME THE IMMACULATE BREAD OF GOD, THE HOST MUST BE SEPARATED FROM ALL THINGS AND KEPT FOR HIM ALONE. THERE IS NO SANCTITY WITHOUT THIS TOTAL DETACHMENT.

XXX

SANCTI ERUNT DEO SUO[1]

THEY SHALL BE HOLY TO THEIR GOD

Lo, the hour of the Sacrifice is here, the Sacrifice of Jesus, my Sacrifice. My soul having been washed in the tears of contrition and exercised in its faith in the sublime mystery, it is now to perform the great act of love which is the Holy Sacrifice: in union with Jesus, Priest and Victim of this Sacrifice, it will offer Him up; thereby giving all honor and glory to the Thrice holy God.

The bread and wine are here upon the altar. As yet they are only the matter of the Sacrifice; but I, a priest of Jesus, by virtue of the mandate of His Church which consecrates me His minister, shall sever them from all profane purposes and make of them a gift of homage unto God; they shall be clothed again in their first holiness, until the power of the Most High deprive them of their own substance to substitute therefore the very substance of Jesus Christ, Son of God.

Meanwhile the Church sings: *"The priests of the Lord offer incense and loaves to God and therefore they shall be holy to their God and shall not defile His Name"*[2] Ah, think on this!...

Whoever thou be, *O man of God*,[3] whom the Lord predestined in His love, by a choice wholly unmerited, to participate in the priesthood of Jesus Christ; whoever thou be, faithful soul, who by thy Baptism sharest, although to a lesser degree, in this sacred office, meditate frequently on this *offertory;* draw thy conclusion and live accordingly.

I am a *priest of the Lord;* I must remind myself of this fact every day, every moment of the day, at home or abroad, toiling and ministering. I am His priest, predestined to this astonishing vocation from all eternity, called by a loving glance which ever follows me, which will follow me forever and ever.

---

1 *Offertory* of Corpus Christi.   2 Lev. 21: 6. *Offertory.*   3 1 Tim. 6: 11.

I am His priest, marked as such even in the very depths of my being with an indelible, an indestructible character, stamped with a seal that likens me to Jesus Christ, the eternal Priest.

Even though I did not wish, even though I ceased to wish, still and forever I should be the priest of the Lord. Must not the knowledge, the consciousness, of this truth be the supreme torment in hell for one who has proved unfaithful, for the apostate, the perjurer?

Are there not critical junctures in the life of a priest when the recollection of this truth becomes a necessity? And not only a necessity, but a source of strength, too, an honor, a victory, and withal a glory rendered to God!

A *priest of the Lord, I make oblation to God*. That is the priestly attitude which is proper above all to Jesus Christ, the *Liturgist* or *Minister of the Holies*,[4] the *Mediator between God and men;*[5] and that is the great vocation of priests, the sublime purpose of their ministry, the supreme dignity of their calling. To this I was predestined, for this I was born, for this chosen; for this I fight, struggle, labor, and suffer; for this I live, yes, for this before all else, above all else: *to make oblation to God*.

I am come to give witness of the Priesthood of Jesus Christ, to offer the unique oblation of the Cross, brought back to the Altar by the power given to me; in my consecrated hands I take up this oblation again and present it before the Face of the Divine Majesty.

If I truly live my vocation, all my thoughts, actions, and energies will be directed toward this daily oblation, toward the *holy mountain* where the saints of God *set up their tabernacles*.[6] If I preserve and cultivate this priestly spirit, wherever I be, whatever I do, or suffer, or accomplish, I shall keep constantly that interior attitude of *one making offering:* I *shall not go out of the sanctuary of the Lord*, but shall remember *that the oil of the holy unction of my God* is as a diadem upon me. *Quia oleum sanctae unctionis Dei sui super eum est*.[7]

I make oblation to Trinity one, to Oneness trine, in order myself to be reunited with this God and to reunite with Him all those in whose name I make oblation as their consecrated mediator.

But I do this only through Jesus Christ, the first Mediator; and the more I act through Him, the more I live in Him, the more I walk with Him, just so

---

4 Heb. 8: 2.   5 1 Tim. 2: 5.   6 Ps. *Judica me*.
7 Because the oil of the holy unction of his God is upon him (Lev. 21: 12).

much the better do I make oblation to the God Who is both One and Three.

To God, through Jesus Christ, I make oblation of *incense and loaves.* The incense, most holy Lord, is Prayer, the great Prayer, the Holy Mass itself, that Prayer which confesses Thy sovereign and absolute rights over me, which adores, gives thanks, supplicates, expiates; and does this not comprehend all religion?

Perhaps the *incense* symbolizes also in some sort the miserable creature that I am, this resin of sin which Thy Priesthood, O Jesus, casts into the brazier of love which is Thy Heart, transforming it into a virginal perfume, into a living and filial confession of Thine Omnipotence and of the nothingness of Thy creature who by his "holy and venerable"[8] hands, offers it up to Thee, the Most High.

The *loaves,* they must be Thyself, Lord Jesus; they must be Thy Church and her children, this holy people, Thy Mystic Body. We are the crushed wheat-grains, which, in the water of Baptism, form the new leaven, *nova conspersio,*[9] and which beneath the action of the fire of the Spirit, form, in all their multitude, with Thee, the unique Bread, the unique Victim of the Sacrifice: the pure oblation which the hands of Thy priests lift up to God on their golden patens. This oblation they envelop with the incense of prayer which is the Mass, in order that every Christian life may be made holy and fragrant with God, in order that this life, directed toward God, may give to the Blessed Trinity all honor and all glory.

And that, to conclude, is why I, more than others, *must become a saint,* one *sanctified in the truth,*[10] a consecrated soul, *offered as a victim,*[11] embodying as fully as possible the Christ Who is soon to be immolated at the altar.

I shall be this *saint* if I comprehend what is happening at the altar, if I imitate the God Whom I shall hold in my hands—*agnoscite quod agitis, imitamini quod tractatis*—if I comprehend and imitate in such fashion that, celebrating the mystery of the death of the Lord, I keep watch and ward over my own members, to make them die to all their vices, to all their concupiscences.[12]

Then shall I be a sacrifice of praise to the Heavenly Father, through

---

8 *Act of Consecration.*   9 1 Cor. 10: 17.   10 John 17: 17.
11 Sense of John 17: 19
12 Understand what you do; imitate what you touch (*Pontificale Romanum:* Rite of Ordination).

Jesus Christ, in the unifying love of the Holy Ghost; then shall I be, both as *offering* and *offered*, "the *incense* whose fragrance of life gives rejoicing to the Church, a *bread of life*, pure and spotless, whose word and example build this house which is the family of God."[13]

I shall be holy for the Church; I shall be holy above all *for my God*. My life, passing into and becoming one with the priestly holiness of Jesus Christ, will become in every one of its acts a new canticle, repeating before the Thrice-Holy Lord the *Sanctus* which shall have no end.

Henceforth I shall have but one care: *never to dishonor the Name of the Lord*, the Name of my Heavenly Father, the Name of Jesus Christ, the Incarnate Word, the eternal Priest according to the order of Melchisedech, the One Who remains forever the perfect and adorable manifestation of the glory of God.

I should dishonor Thy Name, Lord Jesus, Thy Name exalted above all names, if, unfaithful to my vocation, I ceased to make *oblation to God of the incense and the loaves*, in Thee, as Thy saints must; I should dishonor Thy Name if, failing to comprehend the *Mystery of faith*, the paschal mystery renewed each morning at the holy altar, I should refuse to make this *passage*[14] with Thee again, to go by this way which, from the depths of Thy humiliation and self-abnegation, O Son of God, leads upward to exaltation in Thy glory.[15]

In short, I should dishonor Thy Name if my entire life did not reflect Thine, if it did not bear evidence of a state of soul giving through Thee, with Thee, and in Thee, in the Spirit of Love, all honor and all glory to Thy Father. O Jesus Christ, make me Thy saint!

---

13 Ibid. 14 *Pasch* means *passage*. 15 Phil. 2: 9.

XXXI

AD GLORIAM NOMINIS SUI[1]

TO THE GLORY OF HIS NAME

Since my office as priest is to minister at the divine oblation, to offer the incense and the loaves, I must become a saint and must never dishonor the Thrice-Holy Name of my God. Not only every priest but also each one of the faithful must desire, must strive for, this holiness, since, in the Mystical Body of Jesus, each one, according to his capacity and his place in the hierarchy, is priest in union with Jesus Christ, the sublime Priest of the Father.

Now my first, my principal, my essential intention as one offering and as one wishing to be offered in union with my Christ is to give praise and glory to the Name of the Lord, *ad laudem et gloriam Nominis sui.*[2]

To be sure, I shall offer *the spotless Host* unto Thee, *my living and true God,* great Father of all things, *for the expiation of mine own countless sins, offenses, and negligences, and for all here present, as also for all faithful Christians, living or dead, that it may avail for my own and for their salvation unto life eternal,*[3] unto that Life eternal which is Thy Christ, that so we may one day quench our thirst in the torrent of Thine ineffable pleasure; yes, that is just, and right, and necessary; but it is still not the sublime intention of which the Church speaks.

This chalice which I offer unto Thee and upon which Thy glance rests so lovingly is *an odor of sweetness* that rises into the presence of Thy divine Majesty, making supplication before Thy Face *for the salvation of the whole world;*[4] yes, but that, again, is not the supreme, the fundamental intention.

We pray for the benefit of Thy holy Church, which Thou desirest to be ever more and more truly the Body of Thine incomparable Priest and Victim, the Lord Jesus, which Thou desirest to be ever more and more

---

1 Response to the *Orate, Fratres.*   2 To the praise and glory of His Name.
3 Prayer: *Suscipe, Sancte Pater.*   4 Prayer: *Offerimus.*

truly His beloved Spouse for whom He constantly gives Himself; yes, our Sacrifice seeks and implores this benefit, but the intention of intentions, the one which pleases Thee even more, is still more exalted, still more worthy of Thy Name.

O Jesus Christ, Priest and Victim of our oblation, the great object toward which Thy Sacrifice directs itself with fullness of desire, with all sanctity and perfection, is the glory of the adorable Trinity, the glory of the Father, the glory of the Son, the glory of the Holy Ghost, the glory of Trinity in Oneness, the glory of Oneness in Trinity!

Thou desirest that this Sacrifice, the Sacrifice of Thine only-begotten Son and of His Church, acknowledge this glory which is intrinsically Thine, which is Thy life, Thine essence, Thy most holy Being, that it recognize this glory as due unto Thee, as perfect, as impenetrably sublime; Thou desirest that this Sacrifice sing the nothingness of the creature before the indispensable Being of the Creator; Thou desirest that it acknowledge Thy Power, Thy Wisdom, Thy Goodness as having sovereign rights over all that is, all that breathes, all that feels, thinks, loves. Thou desirest that its fragrance rise to the inmost sanctuary of Thine adorable relations, O Holy Trinity, that it pay homage to them, praying that they may be as they were from all eternity, as they now are, as they will be forever, world without end.

It is Thy intention that all there is of glory upon earth, all that adorns, beautifies, and elevates every creature, should rise, through this Sacrifice, in praise unto Thy Holy Name. And though nothing be added thereby to Thine essential glory, Thou desirest nevertheless that this homage return to Thee, the Source of all good, celebrating Thy divine bounteousness. *Gloria Patri, et Filio, et Spiritui Sancto.*[5]

That, therefore, is the superlative intention of my sacrifice, of my oblation to God. Implicit therein is a fearful spoliation of self, an unparalleled detachment, a measureless generosity of soul. Thy glory, O my God, Thy glory alone stills the deep longing of my heart; it empties me of self-seeking, deals death to my ego, makes me a *spotless host*, a most pure bread, worthy of being offered upon the paten which will hold the Body of Thy well-beloved Son.

---

5 Glory be to the Father, and to the Son, and to the Holy Ghost.

I shall pray for the Church, for all the faithful, living and dead, and *for my own welfare*—yes, for that is right and according to Thy designs, Lord. But I shall desire all that only as it is subordinate to Thy praise and Thy glory, in order that Thou be proclaimed God blessed forever and ever.

My God, Father of my Lord Jesus Christ, and my Father, do Thou receive graciously this oblation of ourselves, of myself, *suscipiamur a te, Domine*,[6] this oblation which is permeated with the deep contrition of our sinful, our unworthy souls, and which we dare to present to Thee as a sign of humble self-abasement, *in spiritu humilitatis et in animo contrito*.[7] May it remain the sincere and tender expression of that perfect dependence which keeps us at Thy feet, which acknowledges our nothingness, and becomes a hymn to Thy glory, *et sic fiat sacrificium nostrum*.[8]

Spirit of Sanctity, of all Sanctity, that is to say, of utter dependence upon our God, come, descend upon us, Thou, our Sanctifier. *Veni, Sanctificator!*[9] Thou art the fire from Heaven that rests upon the holocaust; Thou penetratest, burnest, consumest it so utterly that nothing more remains of it than the ashes, a dust which sings Thine all-powerful dominion, *omnipotens aeterne Deus*....[10]

Come, Thou Spirit of fire! Descend suddenly upon us, upon me, now, at this hour of the Sacrifice; inflame, consume me, accomplish within me Thy mystery of detachment, of abnegation, of death to self. Sanctify this Thy matter, in order that, set apart from all things, it may become the pure bread which is offered unto Thy glory at the altar.

Bless Thy victim, whose desire is to be united with Jesus Christ, that he may serve the glory of God's Name, *sacrificium tuo sancto Nomini praeparatum*.[11]

Let Thy purifying flame sweep through my heart and cleanse it of all self-love, so that, being given in entire devotion to the glory of the Holy Trinity, it may return at last to that One from Whom it comes and for Whom alone it was created.

---

6 May we be received by Thee, O Lord.
7 In an humble spirit and a contrite heart.
8 And may our sacrifice so be offered up...
9 Come, O Thou Who makest holy.
10 Almighty, Eternal God.   11 This sacrifice, prepared for Thy Holy Name.

XXXII

PER HUJUS AQUAE ET VINI MYSTERIUM[1]

BY THE MYSTERY OF THIS WATER AND WINE

Whoever would make sacrifice to God of Jesus and of himself must possess a most profound, and entire, and spiritualizing detachment; he must lose himself in Jesus Christ, must disappear in Him.

He, Jesus Christ, is the wine of God His Father; I am but the drop of water which longs to be mingled, which does commingle, with this wine to become one with Him in His Precious Blood. O mystery! And beneath this mystery it is that I, divested of self, make oblation unto God of Jesus and of myself.

This mystery is rooted deeply within Thee, O my Saviour, Word of God, incarnate for me. For does not this mingling of the wine and water in the holy Sacrifice bring to mind that ineffable personal union of the Word, Which Thou art, with Thy sacred Humanity? O divine Nature, Thou art the wine of God; Thou, O holy Humanity, art the water, symbolic of the creature. The wine and the water, without losing their identity, have been blended into Thine adorable Being, into the God-Man. But in this miracle of miracles—never again to be wrought!—Thou consentest that we become happy participants in our own fashion and in the degree possible to us. Thou grantest, O Jesus Christ, that, *by the mystery of this water and wine, we be made partakers of His divinity*—so rich—*Who vouchsafed to become partaker of our humanity*—so poor.[2] Ah, to these heights Thy sanctifying grace would lift me and there uphold me!

The very fact of my creation was *a thing so wondrous:* my recreation in Thee and by Thee, Lord Jesus, is more *marvelous* still by far. For lo, my Baptism engrafts me on Thee, Vine of the elect; I am become a branch of Thee, drawing from Thy divine stock and drinking the sap which gives it

---

1 Prayer: *Deus, qui humanae substantiae,* O God, Who in creating human nature....
2 *Ibid.*

Christian life. O Mystery of the saints of Jesus!

All things I hold in common with Thee, Lord Jesus; all Thy Mysteries are bestowed upon me, are mine own: by Thy grace I live them. When Thou didst first enact them, in the sojourn Thou madest on this earth to realize them, I was in Thee; I was in Thee when Thou wast conceived in the womb of a Virgin Mother; when Thou livedst Thine ineffable secret and hidden life; when Thou wast baptized in the river Jordan by the greatest of the sons of women; when Thou didst preach the Kingdom of God; when Thou sufferedst agony, wast scourged, crowned with thorns, when Thou expiredst in the *Consummatum est*[3] of the Cross; when, gloriously, Thou didst take up Thy life again, and then didst make Thine astonishing ascent to Thy heavenly throne. My Baptism has given me a share in all these Mysteries. What grandeur, what sublimity, what divinity I attain in Thee, Lord Jesus!

Therefore, never do I come before Thine altar to renew there the Work of Thy Redemption without being thus poured, water of earth as I am, into Thee, the wine of Heaven, without being completely divested of self, and ever more perfectly transfused into Thine eternal Priest!

"I am the little drop of water which the wine of the Mass absorbs. And the wine of the Mass becomes the Blood of the God-Man, Who is substantially united to the Most Holy Trinity. The little drop of water is borne away, therefore, into the river of Life of the Holy Trinity. Will it ever be pure enough, clear enough, this little drop of water destined to have a part in the Holy Sacrifice of the Mass?"[4]

Receive, O Holy Trinity, this oblation which we make to Thee, which I make to Thee, in memory of the Mysteries of Our Lord Jesus Christ, in honor of Mary and of all the saints, who have entered into them as no one else; would that I also might be forever lost to sight therein this morning, like a drop of water!

Saints of Jesus, intercede for us! Intercede for me, that, like you, I may become pure praise at this august Sacrifice which casts me thus into the Chalice of the Lord!

---

[3] John 19: 30.   [4] Cardinal Mercier.

XXXIII

ORATIO MEA SICUT INCENSUM

LET MY PRAYER BE DIRECTED AS INCENSE

The great Prayer of the priest of the Lord, the Prayer of the people surrounding him in this solemn moment, is the Sacrifice itself. It is prepared; the gift of sacrifice to God has undergone a preliminary sanctification. In a little while it will be no other than Jesus Christ Himself, the divine and substantial Prayer of the saints. I beseech the Heavenly Father that I may send this living Prayer up to Him like an incense, like the incense which rises from the glowing fire of the censer. Lord, *let my prayer,* which will soon be Thy Dearly-beloved Himself, *be directed as incense in Thy sight!*

The censer is my heart, my priestly heart. Ah, more precious is it far, O my God, than the golden or silver censers which Thy children swing at the foot of Thine altars. This censer was once, I know, a formless, impure thing, wholly defiled. But Thy grace made of it in Baptism the receptacle of Thy love which burns therein, which should consume glowing coals therein. My God, I offer Thee this censer which is my heart; it is not worthy of Thine infinite purity, but consider that within it burns Thine own fire, that Fire which Jesus, the High Priest, came to cast on the earth and with which He wills that it be kindled.[1]

Spirit of Jesus, High Priest of the Father, blow upon this Fire which Thou art; blow on it as a mighty wind, *Spiritus vehemens,*[2] as Thou blewest on the solemn day of Thy Pentecost. Rekindle with Thy breath this Fire already, mayhap, extinguished; this Fire smoldering, at least, beneath my ashes, the ashes of nothingness. O God of Love, light the boundless conflagration of Thy Charity, that we may cast therein the incense that rises to Thy very throne, to the sublime altar of Thy Majesty!

This sacred incense is the symbol of my Prayer, or, rather, of the Prayer

---

1 Luke 12: 49.
2 Wonderful are the surges of the sea: wonderful is the Lord on high (Ps. 92: 4).

I ought to offer, ought, I should say to *be,* in order to rise to such heights, into the every presence of my Heavenly Father.

So high must one mount, so high must one be in order to offer the Divine Sacrifice! And only Thy Prayer can lift me up to the wonderful heights of the vast ocean which is the Lord, *mirabiles elationes maris, mirabilis in altis Dominus.*[3]

As I was saying, Thou, O Jesus Christ, art this Prayer, this living Orison of the saints; this Prayer is Thyself in me, myself in Thee; it is Thyself and myself realizing the unity of the priesthood at the altar, where by Thy will I rise with Thee into Thy Father, into God.

Lord, cast Thou me into the brazier of Thy Love, of Thy Holy Spirit. Oh, that my soul, like incense sweetly fragrant, might this moment make its ascent with Thee into God, *ascensio mentis in Deum,*[4] its ascent into Thy Father! Oh, might it, like incense, like the *smoke of perfumes* rising from the censer of Thy holy Angel;[5] ascend in the whiteness of innocence the steep height of Thy Heaven and appear to Thy delight before Thy Face, O God of all beauty, O God of all sweetness, O God of all sanctity!

No, there is no Prayer comparable to the Holy Mass; it is a series of steps mounting ever higher and higher that lead us to perfect charity and, thereby, to union with the Thrice-blessed Lord.

O Jesus, let my Prayer, that is to say, Thy Sacrifice and mine—Thy glorious Humanity and my own so miserable humanity united to Thine and fused into a oneness of Love—rise like the incense from my censer, whose fire Thou, O Jesus Christ, shalt enkindle to a glowing ardor!

---

3 Acts 2: 2.   4 Elevation of the mind to God (St Thomas, defining prayer).
5 *Offertory* of Michaelmas.

XXXIV

LAVABO INTER INNOCENTES MANUS

I WILL WASH MY HANDS AMONG THE INNOCENT

O Jesus, in this supreme moment, when Thou art about to lead me into Thy Holy of Holies, into which Thou permittest me to enter, me, a wretched creature, yet cleansed by Baptismal grace and subsequently resplendent with the merciful effects of Thy loving-kindness, in this moment I purify my hands, which I would might be as holy as Thine own, O Jesus, Who art the Sovereign and Sublime Priest of this Sacrifice, the spotless Victim Who makest all Heaven to bend down over this altar!

Thy hands, *holy and venerable*,[1] from this moment sanctify my own. I can now lift them up to God, Thy Father and mine, and sing the Prayer, the Orison which Thou art, O Jesus, the only one which can transport us into Him: now I can *compass Thine altar* and minister thereat with awe and adoration, can *tell of all Thy wondrous works, universa mirabilia*....

Yes, Thine altar will become for me this morning a *veritable tent wherein I shall contemplate Thy glory: a tabernacle*, O Jesus, the adorable wound in Thy side, to which I shall entrust my soul, that it may never stray into the tents of the wicked, nor have part with any who profane Thy Holy Blood.

O King of Virgins, Purity of Angels, Splendor undimmed of the Face of the Father, so that *whoever seeth Thee, seeth the Father*,[2] Thou art my innocence. I enter into Thee, Lord Jesus, I, Thy wholly unworthy minister, *Ego autem in innocentia mea ingressus sum.*[3] I wish to be so truly united with Thee, to enter, to penetrate Thy being so perfectly, to disappear in Thee so totally, that no creature, not even an angel, would be able to see me more. So completely hidden in Thy sacerdotal dignity must we be, Lord, we Thy priests, in order to hold in our hands the spotless Host, the pure and holy Victim which Thou art, Thou God of innocence!

---

1 *Canon* of the Mass.   2 John 14: 9.
3 But I have walked in mine innocence.

Therefore I pray Thee, I supplicate Thee a last time: Redeem me again today and have mercy on me, *redime me et miserere mei!*[4] Once more let the cleansing power of Thy plenteous Redemption flow into my soul, into my body, into my entire being. I cry out to Thee in all humility and sincerity: Remember Thine august and bloody Sacrifice of the Cross; remember Thy most holy wounds, from which flowed the most Precious Blood which cleanses the world, which, if need were, would cleanse a thousand worlds; remember Thy *strong cry and Thy tears*,[5] O Jesus, which moved to sorrow the poor thief's heart, till then so obdurate; *redime me et miserere*, redeem Thy creature once more and be ever merciful to me and to all Thy priests who, at this moment, are preparing to immolate and offer up the sacrifice of praise.

May this redemption bestowed upon our souls establish us in the rectitude which honors Thee, in that rectitude which is nothing other than Thy sanctity, Lord Jesus, in that rectitude with which Thou troddest the dolorous way of Thy Passion, and which gave so great glory to God. *Pes meus stetit in directo.*[6]

May this people surrounding us be so uplifted spiritually by our example that it also, drawn by the fragrance of holiness in Thy priests, shall determine likewise to climb the hard and stony heights of Thy Calvary, represented by Thine altar. And may Thy Father thus be glorified in the assemblies of the faithful, *in ecclesiis benedicam te, Domine.*[7]

---

4 Redeem me, and have mercy on me.
5 Hebr. 5: 7.
6 My foot hath stood in the straight way.
7 In the churches I will bless Thee, O Lord.

XXXV

UNITATIS ET PACIS DONA[1]

THE GIFTS OF UNITY AND GRACE

The great gift of God is the Bread come down from Heaven, the Wine changed into the Blood of Christ. In these we behold the sublime Victim and about to be offered at the altar to appease God and to nourish us.

This Bread is One, this Wine is One; here they are on the paten, in my chalice. I offer them in their unity, for it is in this unity that they please God and are pledges of peace to me. One in this host, one in this wine, is a multiplicity, a throng which I see, and contemplate, and admire, because I see it, and contemplate it, and admire it as it appears to me blended into the unity of the bread and of the wine of God.

For, in fact, what I admire in this bread, in this white and immaculate host, is a composite of little grains, ground, blended, and pressed together into the finest flour, which, after being combined with water and kneaded, became a single mixture, a dough which fire has purified and made my bread of sacrifice.

Sacred symbol of Christian unity! We are the little grains of wheat; crushed beneath the millstone of contrition, we were cast into the Baptismal waters in order to enter as one compact body into the unity of Christ; a new dough, detached from all things, we became, beneath the fire of the Holy Spirit, this same Christ; with Him, we are the spotless Host. Many grains have made the one Bread of Sacrifice.

In like manner, this wine with its celestial fragrance is made from many grapes, the juices of which commingled to produce this divine liquid, this one libation to the Lord God. We are the grapes that become one in Jesus.

It is this most excellent Bread which I have just offered; it is this most

---

1 *Secret* of Corpus Christi.

rare Wine which I present to the gaze of the Heavenly Father; and in this Bread, and in this Wine also, I shall see Jesus and all who are His. Behold, these are the gifts of unity, these are the gifts of peace, the fruit thereof. In the *cor unum et anima una*[2] we give ourselves to the service of God; and here is implied a final detachment, in that, torn from our egotistic self-worship, we are fused into the incomparable fellowship of the body of Christ.

Unus panis, unus corpus, multi sumus, omnes.[3] Behold us all, one Bread as we are, now one Body in Jesus Christ, the ineffable bond of Christian unity, "the greatest of all possessions."[4]

What unity and peace, what perfect incorporation, what wonderful communion! *O Lord, grant to Thy Church the gifts of unity and peace, which are mystically shown forth in the offerings we make to Thee.* Vouchsafe that we may ever be united to our Christ, to all our brethren, in this oblation which glorifies Thee!

Give to all whom Thou hast united, like the wheat and the fruit of the vine, into one single body to remain forever united in one spirit also, in order to be offered thus to God and to realize the prayer of supreme Love: *Ut unum sint!*[5]

May this unity, which is the inexhaustible source of peace for Thy Church, be *the incense which rises as prayer unto Thee*[6] and make fragrant the gifts which we consecrate to Thee. May it make us *Thine innocent*, those who with *pure hands* may compass Thine altar. May it *separate us from the wicked and deliver us from their death*. May we, Lord, glorifying Thee in this unity, remain in the straight way which leads to the eternal dwelling of Thy Glory, *locum habitationis gloriae tuae!*[7]

---

2 One heart and one soul (Acts 4: 32).
3 For we, being many, are one bread, one body, all.... (1 Cor. 10: 17).
4 St Ignatius of Antioch to the Ephesians.
5 That they may be one (John 17: 21).
6 The incensing at the *Offertory*.
7 The place where Thy glory dwelleth (Ps. *Lavabo*).

OBLATION OF THE VICTIM

From the Preface to the Our Father

THE LOVE WHICH HAS WROUGHT DETACHMENT NOW ASPIRES TO MAKE THE SOUL A COMPLETE SACRIFICE. IT MUST DIE IN ORDER TO LIVE; IT MUST BE TRANSFORMED INTO THE LOVED OBJECT; THEREFORE LOVE REPRODUCES IN IT THE DEATH OF THE LORD JESUS.

XXXVI

SURSUM CORDA

LIFT UP YOUR HEARTS

Behold us now entered upon the *Mystery of the great Action;*[1] from now on we are face to face with our God, with God the Father almighty, the Lord God, holy and eternal. He is drawing us to Him. Who is oblivious of it? A voice cries: *Sursum corda*, lift up your hearts, forsake the earth, and enter into the Lord, your God.

Sursum corda! This voice calling me—whose voice is it but Thine, Lord Jesus, Thou universal Mediator between Heaven and earth, whose but Thine, inviting me to be lifted up to Thee, my Priest and my Victim, to be lifted up to this Holy Cross from which—as Thou saidst—Thou drawest all things to Thyself,[2] and to which Thou enticest myself?

Sursum corda! Leave behind the earth, O my soul, stretch thine arms up toward the heights where Thy supreme Pontiff, Jesus Christ, holds sway over all creation and whence He calls all His creatures unto Him, desiring to unite the whole universe in the mystery of the great Action which renews the Work of Redemption!

Sursum corda! Arise, O my soul, break the bonds thyself that hold thee to things of earth, and let thyself be borne upward by Jesus Christ, the divine Lover Whom thou canst no longer resist.

Sursum corda! Leave behind thee the noxious exhalations of the low valleys of men; hasten to the divine heights to breathe the air of God. Be with Jesus Christ, abide with Jesus Christ, open out thine arms with Jesus Christ! And then, above all, enter into His Heart. See, the wound in His side is wide open and is distending still more with loving desire to let thee enter, thee and all whom thou lovest, to receive thee and thine in His Holy of Holies....

Sursum corda! Yes, in His Holy of Holies.... For even there wilt thou

---

[1] Ancient designation for the Holy Mass.   [2] John 12: 32.

have to penetrate, wilt have to hide thyself, and disappear utterly, if thou desirest at any price to join in the intentions of this Pontiff and be invested with His functions of Priest and Victim in the hour of His ineffable oblation.

Sursum corda! Lift up your hearts! Come, ye creatures of God, all whose mediator I am through Jesus Christ between His Father and you! Come, together let us go to the Cross, together let us hide in His wound, in order that we may be wholly absorbed in His Action and, for a moment at least, live His great Mystery, the Mystery of faith, in which His Blood is shed for the world and its salvation.

Sursum corda! Draw us, draw me to Thee, Lord Jesus! I need to feel in this hour that Thou truly drawest me according to Thy promise. Draw Thou me, Force of the Father, Strength of the Holy Spirit, draw me to Thee by the manifestation of Thy Truth and of the infinite charms contained therein, by Thy hidden sweetnesses, known only to those who taste of them!

Sursum corda! Draw unto Thee my rebellious will, enchain it to Thy holy Cross; bind it fast with the chains of Thy blessed Passion! May it choose in truth to die to all things in order to live for Thee alone! May it choose, and choose irrevocably, to give Thee this real and necessary pledge—its heart's blood mingled with Thine that it may live Thine august mystery.

Sursum corda! Follow, follow, O my soul! He calls thee; resist not, withstand Him no longer. Hasten into the open arms of the Lord Jesus, and there, with Him, alone between Heaven and earth, *fill up those things that are wanting of the sufferings of Christ, for His Church, who is His Body and His fullness.*[3]

Sursum corda! I follow Thee, Lord, *et nunc sequor ex toto corde.*[4]

---

[3] Col. 1: 24.   [4] And now I follow with my whole heart.

XXXVII
GRATIAS AGAMUS
LET US GIVE THANKS

The sacrosanct prayer which is the *Canon*, the prayer which begins, accomplishes, and ends the measureless Mystery of the Consecration, this prayer is a continuous Thanksgiving or Eucharist.[1] No other prayer is worthy of comparison with it: it is in reality the prayer of God, of the divine Priest and Victim of this transcendent Oblation.

How sublime is the *Preface* of the Eucharistic Action, and what glory it offers to God! How it illuminates the august mystery and enkindles the flame of love in the heart of whoever contemplates it!

Gratias agamus. Yes, give thanks, O my soul, to the Lord God, to the Father of thy Lord Jesus Christ, to His Omnipotence, *Pater omnipotens*,[2] to His Holiness, *Domine sancte*,[3] to His Eternity, *aeterne Deus*.[4] For as He is holy, so He conceived the adorable mystery of the Holy Eucharist, heaping therein all the riches and powers of sanctity; as He is omnipotent, so He thus conceived and realized it; as He is everlasting, so He prolongs into endless ages its blessed action in men, who are transformed thereby in Jesus.

Vere dignum et justum est. Yes, it is meet and just, right and availing unto salvation, to give thanks unto Thee, to "hold Eucharist" for the Eucharist, at all times and in all places! Through our thanksgiving Thou renderest us worthy of Thee, O Father; Thou permittest us to fulfill all justice, which in turn consecrates our mutual intercourse; Thou leadest us forth to the work of our salvation. *Vere dignum.*

The great mysteries of Thy Godhead, divined, discovered in the contemplation of Thy creation, seemed themselves to be lights of such dazzling splendor as to be able to reveal Thee to us and pierce the veil of Thy Power, Thy Wisdom, Thy sovereign Goodness. But the *mystery of the*

---

[1] This word, of Greek origin, signifies *thanksgiving*.
[2] Father almighty.   [3] O holy Lord.   [4] Everlasting God.

Incarnation of Thy Word, of Thine Only-Begotten Son, of Truth Itself, of eternal Wisdom, that is *an hitherto unknown ray of Thy divine glory which bursts upon the ravished eyes of my soul.*

Lord Jesus, by an unheard of condescension, in that, having descended to my dust, having placed Thyself within my reach, having consented to empty Thyself of Thy glory and assume the form of my slavery, Thou, here, in this mystery, hast allowed Thyself to be touched, contemplated, and recognized *as over all things,* God blessed forever and ever.[5]

Thy Holy Eucharist is nothing other than Thy sublime Incarnation continued in our midst. And I, therefore, like Thy most holy Mother, like Thy chosen Apostles, like all those who, in the rapturous joy of their hearts, could kiss Thy hands and Thy feet, like Thomas, the privileged one who dared—but Thou wouldst have it so!—to place his whole hand within Thy wounded side, like all these, I myself can see Thee also, can contemplate Thee and adore Thee, can lay at Thy feet all the lowly homage of my faith, and hope, and love.

For in thus disclosing Thyself, though but beneath the appearances of the Sacred Host, *in making Thyself thus visible,* Thou drawest me to the love of things invisible.[6] O Jesus Christ, Whom I believe to be at the right hand of the holy, the almighty, the eternal Father, Thou art nevertheless the divine Invisible to this heart thirsting for the sight of Thee. Yet the Sacred Host partly, no, almost entirely, lifts the veil which conceals Thee from my love. There where Thou art, thither I feel myself drawn, impelled, shall I say; I know Thou art there, and I hold Thee fast, embrace Thee in the arms of my faith, *nil hoc Verbo veritatis verius.*[7]

Lord, increase this faith; give it fresh vigor from the new ray descending from this Sun which Thou art, O Eucharistic God; let me live henceforth only in this light, only by giving thanks, having become forever *Thy Sacrifice of praise.* Amen.

---

5 Rom. 9: 5.   6 *Cf. Preface* for Christmas, which is also that of Corpus Christi.
7 Nothing can be truer than Truth's very Word.

XXXVIII
SANCTUS, SANCTUS, SANCTUS

HOLY, HOLY, HOLY IS THE LORD

Holy, Holy, Holy, that is the hymn of glory which, in eternal jubilation, is sung to Thee, Most Holy Father, by Thine Angels and Archangels, by Thy Thrones and Dominations, in union with the Heavenly Powers, with Thy glowing Cherubim, with Thy Seraphim aflame with love, all prostrate in an adoration that shall have no end. *Sanctus, Sanctus, Sanctus, Dominus Deus Sabaoth.*[1]

They become an abyss before the Abyss which Thou art, a deep of nothingness before the Deep which is All; *deep calleth on deep,*[2] each replying to other, and finding in this intercourse of love the happiness which is their life. Ah, what holiness is here!

All Heaven and earth bow, cast themselves down, sink prostrate *before the living glory* which is God, the glory *which fills them* and which maintains them in their unapproachable splendor. Like the two Cherubim overshadowing the propitiatory of the Ark of the Covenant, they, also, cry out with but one voice: Holy, Holy, Holy is the Lord, the God of hosts.

Hosannah in the highest! Let the cry of exultation break forth from this earth, O my God, even from this earth which I am, even from my dust and ashes let it break forth; let it mount upward, high, higher, ever higher, *sursum,*[3] even to Thy measureless heights; let it penetrate into the Holy of Holies of Thy glory and there become one with the jubilant song which eternally voices Thy praise.

Blessed is He that cometh in the Name of the Lord! Who is this Blessed One? What is His Name? What is His mission? Ah, He is called Jesus Christ, God, blessed forever and ever! He is the Name of God, He, the ineffable, the unceasing Word, uncreated Wisdom! He comes unto us, comes to ac-

---

1 Holy, Holy, Holy, Lord God of Hosts.   2 Ps. 41: 8.   3 Uplifted.

complish anew the Work of His Redemption; He comes to let us share His Mystery; He comes to make us enter into it, to immerse us therein, *that we may be filled unto all the fullness of God.*[4] Then come, O Thou Blessed One, Thou Word Incarnate, Thou Word eternal, Thou Wisdom enravishing, and we will cry unto Thee, *Hosannah in the highest!*

To Thee also I cry, O Jesus Christ, and in the fullness of my faith: *Holy, Holy, Holy,* God Who art blessed, Whose glory fills Heaven and earth! The Holy of the Father, the Holy of the Word, the Holy of the Spirit! I adore Thee, I give Thee thanks; I await the outpouring of Thy power which is about to bestow upon me once more the benefit of Thy sacrifice!

I sink into my nothingness, I efface myself, I disappear in the presence of Thy Beauty. I die to all things to live only to Thy glory, *that that which is mortal in me may be swallowed up by the Life which Thou art,*[5] O Thou Life of the living, divine *destroyer of our death!*[6]

Thou comest to me in the Name of Thy Father! Thy mission is never ended in a soul which must die gradually to itself and be filled little by little with Thy life. Then come Thou again today; come to Thy Calvary, to Thine Altar, to my soul; enter Thou therein as conqueror of death, that Thou mayest establish Thy reign there at last and accomplish therein Thy loving Will.

Holy, Holy, Holy art Thou, Lord God! My soul is faint with longing before Thy courts, awaiting Thee, O God *Who is, and Who was, and Who is to come!*[7]

---

4 Ephes. 3: 19.   5 2 Cor. 5: 4.   6 *Preface* of Easter.   7 Apoc. 1: 8.

XXXIX

PRO ECCLESIA TUA

FOR THY CHURCH

A priest of Jesus, in whatever degree I participate in this priesthood, as victim with Him, I immerse myself in the mystery of God at the altar. Like Jesus on the Cross, I lift heavenwards my hands and my eyes, for I have left behind me this earth, where, for the time being, all things are obscured from my view, my gaze being eagerly intent on things above; *sursum.*[1] *Te igitur clementissime Pater!*[2] O Father most merciful, I cry unto Thee in Jesus Christ.

Then I cast down my eyes again and bow low in humble supplication; I would fain throw myself to the earth before Thee, Thou God so mighty, so infinite! *Supplices te rogamus ac petimus.*[3]

With love and awe I kiss this altar, which, in a moment, will be the throne of divine Wisdom, which I shall adore in all devotion, in a very transport of faith; and I pray, Lord, *for Thy Church,* Holy and Catholic. It is for her I pray Thee to receive and bless these *gifts,* Thine by every right, these *offerings* of our religion, this *Holy Sacrifice,* which bears witness to our absolute dependence upon Thee.

Pro Ecclesia tua.[4] Thy Church—ah, nothing more precious hast Thou, Lord, in Heaven or on earth, after Jesus Christ! Thy Church, the Mystic Body of Thy Well-Beloved, Who is its adorable Head, the Body which lives from Him, for Him, in Him, with Him; Thy Church, Mary, the Saint of saints, and all Thy holy saints; Thy Church Militant, which traverses the valley of tears, the field of arduous battle, in quest of the Eternal City.

Pro Ecclesia tua. Thy Church, that is, again, Thy Sovereign Pontiff, gloriously reigning, member *par excellence* of this Body, source of Catholic unity; and then our Bishop, center of unity in the district of Thine immense

---

1 On high. 2 Wherefore, O most merciful Father.
3 We humbly pray and beseech Thee. 4 For Thy Church.

Church which has fallen to his rule; Thy Church, that is, all who honor the true Faith, following the Catholic belief, which is that of the Apostles.

Pro Ecclesia tua. Above all, it is for Thy Church, Lord, most merciful Father, that I shall offer up today the Sacrifice Which both glorifies Thee and honors her, that I shall offer up myself likewise, dying with Thy sublime Victim to obtain for this Thy Church peace, protection, unity, guidance, all that is necessary, all that will avail to help her toward her eternal destiny.

What abundance of grace! What fruit! Each one of the faithful, in the state of grace, will share therefore in these thousands of Masses being celebrated every day throughout the world![5] Lord, do I think to unite myself with all Thy priests, over all the earth who offer for Thy Church, and therefore for me also, their adoration, their thanksgiving, their petitions, and their expiations?

Ah! that is what I desire to make my most fervent devotion: prayer for Thy Holy Church! That is the devotion that makes great and generous souls; souls who above all things desire to know and see Thy Church as the holy and immaculate Bride of Jesus Christ, to see her beautiful with the beauty of this Christ, powerful in action, victorious in her battles, holy in her priesthood, and wonderful in the sight of the Angels.

Give scope to thy piety, O my soul; be noble, exalted; seek the glory of thy God, the honor of thy Christ, and that above all things else. Thou art the child of the Church; let that be thy most cherished title. Remember this Church, live for her, suffer for her, if need be, give thy life for her; there is no more sublime act in this Sacrifice, wherein Jesus renews His Oblation.

---

5 Estimated at about 350,000.

XL

MEMENTO, DOMINE

BE MINDFUL, O LORD

For Thy Church, Lord, yes, for her above all else, I am about to offer to Thee the Sacrifice which gives Thee honor and praise, *Sacrificium laudis*.[1] How sweet it will be to give this proof of my faith and gratitude to her, to this Mother of mine! For next to Thee, have I not to thank her for every gift which leads me to Heaven?

I have not yet asked Thee, O my God, to remember Thy priest, me, Thine unworthy servant, *indigno famulo tuo*,[2] upon whom this Church is pleased to bestow the very richest fruit of this Sacrifice. But in this I trust myself to Thee, fully confident of Thy care for me. Ah, yes! I desire this fruit, I receive it, I eat of it, I make it the life of my life, the sustenance of my priesthood, the joy of my oblations, the vigor of my apostolate. Thou wilt provide for me, my Saviour. Let my heart be filled with the saving strength of Thy most blessed Passion! If, one day, Thou make me a saint, the glory will be Thine alone, and that sanctity in others for which I have labored will, again, give honor to Thee and to Thy Church. *Pro me indigno famulo tuo.*[3]

In particular, I pray Thee, Lord—it being both my privilege and my duty—to accord the *special fruit* of this Sacrifice to that soul which I see in my thought and in my heart; to that soul which has recommended itself very specially to my prayers and which I have placed on my paten and have let descend into my chalice to make with the oblation of Jesus Christ and mine one single oblation; to that soul which, in order to share in this privilege, has kindly given me an offering, thus glorifying Thee by satisfying the needs of Thy priest from the altar. Lord, have pity on this soul and remember its wants in consideration of its most Christian charity. *Memento, Domine.*

---

1 The Sacrifice of praise.   2 Thine unworthy servant.
3 For me Thine unworthy servant. This is said by the Pope and by Bishops only; but the intention of Holy Church is that all priests should have it in mind.

Ah, how favored will this soul be, and how favored are all those who may hope, during the sublime *Prayer* of the Holy Mass, to be on the lips or in the thought of a priest when he is about to undertake the most awe-inspiring and most sacred of all acts! If we but realized this truth!

Memento, Domine. Remember also, Lord, most merciful Father, and that in the Name of *Our Lord Jesus Christ* Who alone prays unto Thee here—for I am but His minister, who serve Him—remember all who are present during this all powerful *Prayer* and who follow it with the faith and devotion known unto Thee; remember all who believe in Thy Mystery, who make it the center: the axis, the soul of their devotion, of their Christian life.

Remember all those who offer unto Thee this *Sacrifice of praise, Sacrificium laudis,* who make it the sublime expression of their avowal of the utter dependence of their being, *which is not,* upon Thine, O God, Who art *He Who is.*[4]

Remember *them* and *theirs,* all those who are dear to them, with whom they are united in the love of Thy Christ, O Lord; remember all those who make this oblation of Christian unity a means of fusing their hearts more closely than ever in peace and harmony and love.

They cry unto Thee here as those cried at the Cross who believed in Thy Jesus: Redeem us, Lord; be our plenteous redemption, *copiosa redemptio! Save us* for without Thee we perish! *Keep us* in life, in death, in time and in eternity. *Memento, Domine.*

O eternal God, Who truly livest, *aeterno Deo vivo et vero,* remember, finally, all who make their *thanksgiving,* their Eucharistic prayer, through the Body and Blood of Thy Well-beloved!

---

4 Exod. 3: 14.

XLI

COMMUNICANTES

COMMUNICATING

Remembrance of earth and of legitimate earthly affections has occupied my thought for a little; but now the Church Triumphant, in her turn, draws me heavenward, into her bosom, to participate in her feast, for, in very truth, each Holy Mass, commemorating at the altar the Work of the Redemption, is for her a solemn feast.

The Holy Mass, O all ye Saints of God, is your honor and your glory! For in its representation of the sublime Sacrifice of Jesus Christ, your adored Leader, there passes before your eyes the mystery which is the source of your eternal glorification.

The Holy Mass for you is the Blood of your Saviour entreating your glory, showering upon you His strength, making acceptable in the eyes of the Heavenly Father all the rights purchased for your beatitude.

The Holy Mass for you and in your honor is Jesus Christ, the exalted, the incomparable Priest, giving to you who dwell amid the splendors of Heaven participation in His functions as Priest and Victim; it is Jesus Christ enveloping you in the glory He renders to God His Father; increasing, if one may say so, your power of intercession; and receiving you, finally, you, his chosen members, His elect, as co-heirs in the glorious riches of His Priesthood.

And you draw us, you draw me, to you, ye Saints of God, to enjoy your soul-refreshing intercourse. You desire me to be united with you more closely than ever before, now, in this hour of celestial rejoicing, when you bend in ecstasy over the immaculate Host, when you gaze enraptured upon It, recognizing therein the High God Who makes Heaven and earth to tremble.

O Blessed Mary, Virgin and Mother, Mother of my Lord Jesus Christ, what poignant delight is thine when thou seest upon this altar Him Who descends hither to give thee increase of glory through this Most Precious

Blood, the sublime power of which made thee the "Immaculate Conception!"

Holy Apostles of Jesus, holy martyrs of Christ, who bear witness to the Lamb slain in atonement—and ever renewing this atonement—for the sins of the world, I join in your gladness, in your endless exultation! I see you, all of you, clothed in the purple of that Blood which ransomed your lives and made them a glorification of God and a source of our sanctification.

I bespeak your merits, loudly I entreat your prayers; be our safeguard, ye Saints, be my own safeguard: save me from the anger of the most high God, Who, it may well be, discovers in the depths of my being such unworthiness as sullies my soul and hinders the outpouring of His grace at the very moment when Jesus Christ, His Son and my God, is about to appear.

May your protection be my armour, *muniamur auxilio;*[1] may it satisfy God's Justice, incline His Mercy toward me, and extend over me, His poor and wretched creature, the divine tenderness of His Heart of love; and thus may my communion with you, O Saints of the Lord, give me a new purification, a more than ever confident audacity, which, loosing me from my faint-heartedness, will cast me into His arms, there to receive, on the instant, the kiss that distills in the soul that peace which passes all understanding and which remains a foretaste of Heaven.

---

[1] May we be fortified by your help.

XLII

UT PLACATUS ACCIPIAS

THAT THOU RECEIVE GRACIOUSLY

This is the hour of the oblation, of my priestly oblation, by which I shall give testimony unto Thee, Lord, of my bounden duty and make confession of Thy sovereign and absolute rights over my being, *oblationem servitutis*.¹

This is the hour of the solemn oblation of *Thy whole Christian family*, those of its members here grouped about Thine altar, together with all those who make up Thy Holy, Catholic, and Apostolic Church, Thy Church in Heaven, in purgatory, and on earth, s*ed et cunctae familiae tuae*.²

This oblation, Lord, most merciful Father, we offer to Thee through our august Mediator, Jesus Christ, Thy Son and Our Lord, through Him *Whom Thou ever hearest for His reverence in the days of His flesh*³ and of His Sacrifice. Ah, no, never dost Thou repulse Him, never deniest Thou Him! In Him Thou art always well-pleased; Thou receivest Him in Thy fatherly embrace, accordest Him all that He offers Thee, all that He asks of Thee in making His oblation; for His offering, His supplication is Himself, the eternal object of Thy loving delight.

Oh, then, we beseech Thee, through this eternal Priest, graciously to accept this sacred offering: let it be and ever remain for us the source of richest blessings, *benedictam*;⁴ record it in the secret of Thy mercy and endow it with the measureless abundance thereof, *adscriptam*;⁴ make it ratified, approved, confirmed in Heaven, *ratam*;⁴ let it be truly the Sacrifice of our reason adoring Thee in its Faith, *rationabilem*;⁴ let it be also the object of Thy gratification, since it will be Jesus Himself, *acceptabilem*;⁴ let it be the Eucharist, that is the thanksgiving for all Thy gifts.

With Thy Church, threefold and yet one, who with all right is deeply

---

1 This oblation of our service.   2 And of Thy whole family.
3 Heb. 5: 7.   4 Blessed, approved, ratified, reasonable, acceptable.

concerned therein, we supplicate Thee, O Most Holy Father, that Thou wouldst look upon our oblation, that Thou wouldst look down in mercy upon it; that, in union with Thine ineffable Word, Thou wouldst send upon it Thy Holy Spirit to overshadow and fructify it, in order *that this bread and this wine may become for us the Body and Blood of Thy most beloved Son Our Lord and Saviour Jesus Christ,* for us who shall make Him our Victim and our Sustenance, the pledge of forgiveness and of Life eternal, *ut nobis fiat.*[5]

In view of this immeasurable, this unheard of grace, grant us, O Father, grant unto me Thy peace, that gift of Thy loving-kindness! Encompass us, encompass me with this peace, let it enfold me, wrap me round, that with tranquil and confident heart I may *go to the mountain of incense and myrrh,*[6] to the mountain where stands new implanted the Cross of my Redeemer; there, in its shadow, Lord, let me find refuge from Thine anger, protected by that sign of salvation!

Ah, yes, order my days in Thy peace, that is, in Jesus Christ crucified. See me evermore only in Him, on this second Calvary! I am the thief hanging on the gibbet of Golgotha; I cry out to Him, Thy Jesus: *"Lord, remember me when Thou shalt come into Thy kingdom!"*[7] Answering He will say unto me: *"This day thou shalt be with Me in paradise."* So shall I escape eternal death and be admitted into the number of Thine elect. To bestow; on me this grace and this glory is the purpose of the Holy Mass on this day. *Ab aeterna damnatione eripi et in electorum tuorum jubeas grege numerari.*[8]

---

5 That it may become for us, *i.e.*, the Body and Blood of Our Lord.
6 Cant. 4: 6.   7 Luke 23: 42 *ff.*
8 Grant that we be rescued from eternal damnation and counted within the fold of Thine elect.

XLIII

ACCEPIT PANEM

HE TOOK INTO HIS HANDS THE BREAD AND
THE PRECIOUS CHALICE

The wonderful visit which the earth awaits is now at hand: another moment, and *He, Jesus,* will appear to our enraptured gaze. O soul of mine, can it be thou still dost linger here below? Or dost not rather seem to be in Heaven? O wonder of wonders, O goodness divine! He Who sitteth at the right hand of the Father is to be here in my hands, in these sullied creature hands; here He will offer Himself, here He will give Himself! And still I live!

The sublime Sacrifice is beginning: remember, my soul, that He, Jesus Christ, is its High Priest. Thou, O human priest, art but the unworthy minister thereof; thou lendest thy lips, thy hands, thy heart, that is all; not to the Angels, not even to the flaming Seraphim, is it given to know this joy.

Then do Thou set forth, O Jesus, *the Mystery of the great Action:* as for myself, I hide, I disappear, I sink deep in my nothingness, this nothingness about which Thou castest, nevertheless, the garment of Thine omnipotence.

I shall consecrate in Thy name; I shall offer, I shall give; but in Thy name, by virtue of Thine influx, O Strength of the Father, O Priest of His glory!

Qui pridie quam pateretur.[1] On the eve of Thy Passion, at Thy Last Supper, by an act of supreme love, Thou art to spend that love lavishly, O Jesus Christ, Priest, Victim, Altar of Thy Heavenly Father. So hast Thou loved me in this *in finem,*[2] to excess, to the very end, even as far as a God can go.

Tomorrow, on Calvary, Thou wilt offer up Thine infinitely precious life to Him to Whom all His life belongs, even Thy life as perfect Man. To His glory Thou wilt do this, to His perfect glory, to the glory which Thou alone, O Jesus, eternal Priest, art capable of celebrating, of increasing.

---

[1] Who the day before He suffered.   [2] Unto the end (John 13: 1).

Thou wilt make this oblation for our salvation, for mine, for the salvation of all the world; could there then be even one unincluded in the universal power of Thine Action?

This oblation will be veritably a priestly one: of Thine own self Thou wilt offer Thyself, freely, in full liberty, in the hour, in the manner, that Thou wilt, by the power which is Thine of laying down Thy life and of taking it up again; herein lies Thine infinite merit.

Following the symbolic rite of the expiatory sacrifice of Aaron's Priesthood, Thou wilt shed Thine own Blood and make thereof the precious Oblation. For without blood there is no expiation, no remission of sins. Such will be *the one and only Oblation by which Thou perfectest forever them that are sanctified.*[3]

What an oblation, O Christian souls, and how important it is to go more deeply into its meaning! Here, at the Last Supper, Jesus anticipates betrayal, torture, and deicide. No, He would not have us believe that His people's crime is the cause of our salvation. So what does He do? With the same liberty, the same power, the same excessive love that He will manifest tomorrow, invested with the divine sovereignty which disposes of all things, He voluntarily immolates Himself *in advance*. To God, His Father and ours, He makes oblation of His Body and Blood, this time, *according to the rite of Melchisedech,*[4] that is, under the appearances of Bread and Wine, in a *sacrificial rite* directly representative of the bloody sacrifice of the Cross.

Tomorrow will be the actual shedding of His sacred Blood, His actual separation from His adorable Body—the principal immolation which His priestly intention will make an oblation to the Father Who loves us. Here, at the Last Supper, He foreshows this same visible and voluntary priestly oblation in that He immolates Himself in His own hands by a symbolical immolation which, although not the principal one for Him, yet is truly one with that of the Cross; He immolates Himself, and this by an act of consecration which separates *sacramentally* His Body from His Blood; this *mystical* that is, *unbloody* immolation prefigures the actual shedding of His Blood on Calvary, the Blood of which tomorrow He will make oblation; therefore the act He accomplishes at the Last Supper is likewise a true act of oblation.

[3] Heb. 10: 14.   [4] Gen. 14: 18.

O holy, O adorable immolation! Though *figurative*, thou art by no means but a *simple representation* of tomorrow's bloody immolation; thou art a *real immolation:* the oblation, that is, at the hands of the High Priest of the Victim which will be immolated and which will be one with that offered this evening. This oblation of Thine, O Jesus, is not only *representative;* it is a veritable Action, the *act of sacrifice.*

And, behold, the Holy Mass is instituted! What the Last Supper celebrated really as still to be enacted, the Holy Mass now celebrates as fulfilled. But in both cases the figurative immolation is a true *Action,* an act of offering. Jesus Christ Himself, both Priest and Victim, offers Himself therein immolated. O holy Supper! O precious Cross! O divine Altar! All one in one unexampled Love!

XLIV

DEDITQUE DISCIPULIS DICENS: ACCIPITE

AND GAVE TO HIS DISCIPLES, SAYING: TAKE

In Thine excess of love, O Jesus Christ, Thou wilt have Thy disciples, those whom Thou makest Thy ministers, Thy priests, here, to hold in their hands, in their turn, what Thou heldest in Thy holy and venerable hands; what Thou tookest up to immolate, to offer, to break, and distribute, Thou wilt that they also take up in their hands, still fragrant with the priestly ointment, and immolate, offer, break, and distribute! And this until Thou come again; *Donec veniat!*

On the day of my consecration to the holy priesthood, when my Bishop, taking Thy place, imposed his sacred hands upon me, while the whole body of Thine assembled priests, in union with him and with one and the same action, stretched out their hands over me, Thou, Lord Jesus, saidst to me: *hoc facite in meam commemorationem*—do this in commemoration of Me, to announce and repeat My most blessed Passion, to reenact the Work of My Redemption. And then it was that I, likened unto Thee, was made by Thee a priest forever. *Assimilatus Filio Dei manet sacerdos in perpetuum.*[1] So was it spoken of Melchisedech; and what is he compared with a single priest of Jesus Christ?

Then, O Lord Jesus, Thou, divine model of Thy priests, didst entrust to me the work of the priestly sacrifice which Thou hast just accomplished and which is this same mystical, or unbloody, immolation of Thyself. At the altar I put on the Christ of the Last Supper; in Thy place I become the minister of the *great Action:* that is the whole mystery. And what a mystery offered for your faith, O Eucharistic souls!

Tomorrow, on Calvary, will take place the bloody immolation; but it is

---

[1] Likened unto the Son of God, continueth a priest forever (Heb. 7: 3).

contrary to the faith to think that this immolation can be repeated. No, the Lord Jesus *dieth now no more*[2]—He Who arose from the dead and lives forever and ever! His priestly oblation at Golgotha can never be made again, never be repeated by my ministerial oblation, however holy it be. No, His sublime Sacrifice has been consummated; He has *obtained eternal redemption; He hath perfected forever them that are sanctified; He was offered once to exhaust the sins of many.*[3] A sacrifice possessing eternal efficacy can never be repeated; it would be an offense against Christ, the perpetual Victim, *Hostia perpetua!*[4]

Nor is it possible to conceive of another oblation, priestly and quite ministerial, parallel to His, independent of it, and adding to its value. Never will there be more than the one Priest of the Father, more than one Victim, more than the one Altar; He is all these, He alone, the Christ Jesus!

But His Sacrifice of the Cross can truly subsist still in other oblations as numerous as I may desire. As a priest consecrated by His Church, I become His minister; I act in His place, in His Name as the member of the Christ, High Priest of this ministerial oblation. I make this oblation, but I make it only by virtue of His bloody oblation, which is first, foremost, unique among all, and from which my own derives all its efficacy, being as if incorporated therewith. To this unique oblation, my own adds nothing; no, it simply becomes one with it, being at the same time, however, itself an immolation, a true oblation. That, in sum, is the Holy Mass which I celebrate, or at which I assist, every day.

The Eucharistic Sacrifice offered at the altar is, consequently, an oblation which is one with that of the Cross, and this by reason of the ever-during power of the latter, the power of Christ, which is essentially and eternally sanctifying to the souls which it thus unites to God.

For, in truth, Jesus retains, amid the splendors of the saints, in the Heaven of His glory, His character and existence as perpetual Victim, *Hostia perpetua:* constantly, now, *He appears in the presence of God for us,*[5] showing to Him His divine wounds, the one in His side, too, all irrefragable witnesses to His continual self-offering, witnesses to the *Lamb forever slain.*[6] There He ever intercedes with the Father for us and obtains for His elect, who are the fruits of His Sacrifice, entrance into the glory of Heaven.

[2] Rom. 6: 8.   [3] Heb. 9: 12 and 28; also 10: 14.
[4] St Thomas.   [5] Heb. 9: 24.   [6] Apoc. 5: 6.

But I, armed with His powers, consecrated by His Church, who invests His priests, I, beneath the eternal and living influx of His priesthood, accomplish at the altar a priestly rite of oblation which is representative of that of Calvary. There He poured forth His Precious Blood, separating it from His Body: this was His bloody immolation. Freely He shed His Blood, voluntarily, by His own power, expressing thus outwardly His inner Sacrifice: this was His oblation. Here at the altar, I, exercising His function as Priest and Victim, accomplish an action, a rite, of unbloody immolation and of oblation, a rite representative of the shedding of His Blood, of the separation of His Body and His Blood, and this by the double, separate Consecration. This rite makes a ministerial oblation of the same immolation of the Cross: and therefore it establishes a sacrifice which is real, awe-inspiring, and most holy.

And that is my priestly vocation, which gives me power over the Body of Jesus and over His Blood. What a Mystery, a Mystery of Love!

St Thomas, who sings the praise of the Holy Eucharist, thus proclaimed it: "In as much as this mystery *represents* the Passion of Christ, it has the quality of a sacrifice." And again: "This mystery is *directly representative of the Lord's Passion*, by which Christ, as *Priest* and as *Victim, offered Himself* to God on the altar of the Cross. As for the Victim offered by the priest, it is *one* with that offered by Christ, *one* by a real identity, for it actually contains Christ; as for the priest who offers, he is not one with Christ by a real identity; he must consequently be so by representation. And, therefore, when he consecrates in the person of Christ, he pronounces the consecrating words in the Name of this Christ, lest the Victim appear to be other than the one Jesus held in His hands. That is also why it is better for him to say: 'This is my Body,' than, 'This is the body of Christ.'"

Shall one say then that Christ is every day still crucified, slain? Ah, no. These terms designate only the crime committed against Thee by the Jews, O Jesus, not what is done each morning at the altar. But what Thou wast, there, on Calvary, in the eyes of Thy Father, in Thy role as Priest and Victim, sacrificing, offering, that, we do, believe Thou becomest again each day. For "this Victim is perpetual; once was it offered by Christ, and in such wise that it may be offered every day by His members."[7] What depth of

---

[7] St Thomas.

meaning, yet what simplicity! Christ Himself, He of the Last Supper, He of the Cross, deigns to appear at the altar in His priest! And I, I am this priest, O Jesus, I, Thine unworthy servant! *Quid retribuam?*[8]

---

[8] What return shall I make?

XLV

HOC EST ENIM CORPUS MEUM

THIS IS MY BODY

And the miracle is wrought! *Credo, Domine.* And Thou art in my hands! Thou only holy, Thou only Lord, Thou only Most High, O Jesus Christ! *Credo, Domine.*

I kneel as if overwhelmed, reduced to nothingness before this Mystery. Take heart, priest of Jesus! Arise, lift up thy God! "With thy two hands, which have become His throne, lift Him up before the adoring gaze of the people around thee, before purgatory deeply longing, before Heaven in ecstasy. O Jesus Christ, Thine excessive love bursts forth in new splendor! But it is too much for my weakness; my courage fails, *quia te contemplans totum deficit.*[1]

Adoro te. I adore Thee, Lord Jesus, I can do only that, adore. To adore Thee is to fall silent, to descend into my nothingness, to let myself, my nothingness, be bound at Thy feet in mute confession of wonder.

Lord, I believe all that Thou hast said, Thou, Word of Truth! *Credo quidquid dixit.* I believe even in this total darkness into which my faith casts me: for in this unfathomable mystery of endless love, nothing is offered to the sight, nothing to the touch, nothing to the taste. Ah, if I could see Thee, my eyes in Thine! If I could touch Thee like the little children who were wont to cling to Thee! If I could taste Thy sweetness, O Bread That possessest all sweetness! *Visus, gustus, tactus, in te fallitur.*[2] But no, faith itself, the faith of mine desires not that my demands be satisfied, even the demands of my love. *Credo quidquid dixit Dei Filius.*[3]

I have heard Thy lips utter the Truth: that suffices my faith, suffices all my love, since I can give Thee proof of no surer faith, no greater love than

---

1 For in contemplating Thee it wholly fails (St Thomas: *Adoro te*).
2 Seeing, touching, tasting, all are here deceived (*Ibid.*).
3 I believe whatever God's own Son averred (*Ibid.*).

by trusting myself with complete abandonment to Thy truth; *sed auditu solo tuto creditur!*[4]

In this hour of the solemn Sacrifice which Thy love reenacts, now when my faith is reiterating to me that Thou layest down Thy life, that Thou offerest Thyself, I no longer even see Thy Humanity. Even if I should, even if I should see Thy Blood streaming from Thy Sacred Wounds, like so many fountains for the refreshment of Thy saints, I should believe no more firmly in it, nor more firmly in the God Thou art, O Jesus Christ. *Ambo tamen credens atque confitens.*[5]

Remember me, Lord! Memento mei, Domine! I cry out to Thee like the thief, like the good and penitent thief, taken down from his cross after having already gone with Thee into Paradise. I have taken his place, I, Thy priest, for I must share Thy blessed Passion in order to obtain for souls, for my own soul, too, a part in Thy heavenly kingdom, *quod petivit latro poenitens.*[6]

The adorable wound in Thine opened side, this priceless treasure which Thou hast left me from which to pay my debts, this sure place of refuge whither Thou invitest me to flee continually that I may abide in Thee, and Thou in me, Lord Jesus, this wound, ah, I see it not. Thou knowest this torture of my heart. Thomas was more fortunate than I. But what matter! Like him I cry out to Thee, my hand placed in Thy wide-open side: *My Lord and my God!* Increase my faith, be my one hope, and let me henceforth love only Thee! *Fac me tibi semper magis credere.*[7]

I adore Thee, O living Bread, That givest life to man! Grant to my soul to live only by Thee; give it relish only for Thee and distaste for all that is not Thyself here below. *Et te illi semper dulce sapere.*[8] *Et procidens, adoravit eum.* And the one cured of his blindness, falling down, adored Him.[9]

---

[4] But by hearing only safely 'tis believed (*Ibid.*).
[5] But in both believing and confessing, Lord (*Ibid.*).
[6] What the dying thief of Thee implored (*Ibid.*).
[7] Grant this faith in me may evermore increase (*Ibid.*).
[8] And Thy taste of all things to it sweetest be (*Ibid.*).
[9] John 9: 38.

XLVI

HIC EST CALIX SANGUINIS MEI

THIS IS THE CHALICE OF MY BLOOD

Blood of Jesus, Blood of Calvary *which crieth* to the Father *infinitely better than that of Abel*,[1] I adore thee, overcome by this excess of love.

Love exceeding all bounds! Even on Mount Thabor, amid the splendor of Thy Transfiguration,[2] Thou didst speak of it, O Jesus Christ, to Thy two prophets, before the ravished gaze of Thy chosen Apostles!

Love surpassing all understanding! Thou gavest proof thereof on Golgotha! A chalice there was which at any price Thou desiredst to drink![3] A Baptism Thou hadst wherewith Thou desiredst to be baptized, and how wast Thou straitened until it was accomplished![4] It was the chalice, it was the Baptism of Thy Blood. Thou didst drink this chalice, Thou wast baptized with this Blood. This Blood of Thy chalice, of Thy Baptism, I adore here at Thine altar, where it flows afresh to reenact and commemorate Thy sublime *Sacrifice*. A new excess of love!

Here, Thou art still both Priest and Victim and upon Thyself, O Sacred Humanity of my God, Thou pourest forth, as upon a sublime altar, the great price[5] of salvation, Thy Precious Blood. Toward Thee, O Father, I lift it up in my trembling hands, in hands made holy and venerable by my union with Thy Well-beloved Son, and I adore it. With Thy saints in Heaven, who are clothed in its purple as in a mantle of glory, with Thy saints in purgatory, who bathe therein for their purification, with Thy saints on earth, whose one hope it is, I adore it. O Most Precious Blood of Jesus Christ, unto thee be adoration, and blessing, and glory! Thou are the great price of the marvelous Combat between Life and Death,[6] where the King of Life reigns, living forever!

---

1 Heb. 12: 24.   2 Luke 9: 31. Latin *excessus*, decease.
3 Matt. 10: 38.   4 Luke 12: 50.   5 1 Cor. 6: 20.
6 *Sequence* of Easter Sunday.

Here on earth Thou madest no covenant without blood; Thou laidest upon the children of Israel the obligation to seal that alliance with their blood soon after birth. Thine own people, the holy people of Thy Church, of this Body whose Head Thou art, these Thou dispensest therefrom; instead, Thou wilt shed this Blood, Thou alone—this priceless Blood of Thine—the Blood of the new covenant which establishes peace between earth and Heaven, between man, whom Thou redeemest at this great price, and Thy Father.

O sublime Mystery of faith! Mysterium fidei! This Blood still flows, has not ceased to flow since the hour of the Sacrifice of the Cross! It was flowing before Thy death; it flowed after Thy *Consummatum est,* when Longinus pierced Thy side, opening the blessed Fountain of Thy Heart. If I will, I may put my lips to this spring and quench my thirst in the torrent of Thy love. O mystery! Mystery of faith!

I believe, Lord Jesus! I abandon myself to this faith which sanctifies and saves me. Increase my faith, in order that I may be all the more receptive to the holy influence within me of Thy Most Precious Blood.

Flow, then, O Blood of Jesus, flow over us, over me, *over many,* which is to say, over all who will believe in this Blood and who place their hope therein! Flow through the whole universe, that sin may be washed away, forgiven, expiated, and that every soul may be new-clothed in Him Who is Thy source, the Lord Jesus Christ.

O Pelican full of tenderness, *Pie Pellicane, Jesu Domine,* Thou nourishest our souls with Thine own Blood, though Thou diest for it, with Thy Precious Blood, one drop of which is enough to obliterate the foulest crimes. Then do Thou let fall upon my soul this single drop, that at its contact there may be enkindled within me the great fire of Thy love, so that I also henceforth may be in anguish till this martyrdom be accomplished. Amen.

XLVII

HAEC FACIETIS

YE SHALL DO THESE THINGS

The Sacrifice is accomplished. Once more the memory of the Passion, of Thy blessed Passion, O Jesus, has been celebrated: Thou hast immolated and offered Thyself; the Work of Thy Redemption has been fulfilled and has been applied to our souls, to my soul. Ah, what mystery of death which brings forth Life! Yet it will not yield this highest fruit unless I, priest of Christ, imitate what I have just touched. *Imitamini quod tractatis.*[1]

The virtue of the Holy Mass is that it makes of me, too, one crucified, after the example of Jesus, makes me a Christian entering into the mystery of this death which is the source of Life. *Imitamini quod tractatis.* Only on this condition shall I attain to sanctity, gain any virtue, or obtain any influence over souls: I must die to everything, above all to myself. Within me, also, a separation must be effected, a separation from myself, and my heart's blood must flow over the ruins of my "ego." O precious death, death of the Saints of the Lamb!

Transubstantiation is a program for the priestly and Christian life. So long as I do not pass over into Jesus Christ, what am I? Nothing. The bread and the wine disappear; of their substance nothing remains, really, absolutely nothing; there is no longer anything but fragile, evanescent appearances, doomed to destruction. No, I must let these recreating words be pronounced over my entire being; then will they, transforming me, make of my "ego" the victim, the sacrifice of Christ.

Thou wilt not go so far, O Jesus Christ, as to take from me my human substance, my purely human nature, weak and subject to death. No; and yet for what wondrous assimilation to Thee has Thy Sacrifice prepared me! *The old Adam in me* Thou wilt have no longer: Thou desirest that I put on

---

[1] *Pontificale Romanum:* Rite of Ordination.

Thyself, *a new man;*[2] yes, that I pass over into Thee; *that that which is mortal may be swallowed up by Life;*[3] that the human may put on the divine; that, in brief, *I may live, now not I, but Thou in me.*[4]

It is necessary that I, or, rather, Thou in me—that is understood—be and remain the *perpetual victim*. A priest of Jesus, a believer in him, can be nothing else if he really lives his priesthood. I, too, then, must stretch out my arms on this cross that I may be always in the attitude of prayer which is fitting to my great vocation.

Omnia traham ad meipsum.[5] Then I, also, shall draw all to myself, that is, to Thee, O Jesus Christ, Priest and Victim, to Thee in me; to Thee I shall draw all souls then. So shall I do a work of life[6] for having consented to imitate what I touch, for having desired *to know Thee, O Christ, Thee and the power of Thy Resurrection, and the fellowship of Thy sufferings, being made conformable to Thy death, if by any means I may attain to the resurrection which is from the dead.*[7]

This is the true fruit of the Holy Mass, the real fruit of this consecration which, solemnly representing and announcing the death of the Lord, initiates into its mystery all who have resolved to prolong it in their lives.

Then consecrate us, consecrate me, O Jesus Christ, in memory of us, in memory of me, as I have just done in memory of Thee! The answer of love! *Haec quotiescumque feceritis, in mei memoriam facietis.*[8]

---

2 Col. 3: 9.   3 2 Cor. 5: 4.   4 Gal. 2: 20.
5 I will draw all things to Myself (John 12: 32).
6 2 Cor. 4: 10–12.   7 Phil. 3: 10–11.
8 As often as ye do these things, ye shall do them m memory of Me.

XLVIII

UNDE ET MEMORES

WHEREFORE, CALLING TO MIND

Now that Jesus Christ, the Victim of the Father, has been immolated, the Church, by the ministry of her anointed priest, in union with the sublime intentions of this most holy Victim—self-offered—makes oblation of Him unto the Majesty of God. Recalling the divine mission appointed unto her, she bears up to Heaven with adoring love Him who is her Victim.

And it is I myself, Lord Jesus, who thus bear Thee up to the very throne of Thy Father, I, Thine unworthy servant! But my unworthiness I conceal in Thine own offering; I conceal it there with the gift here present, which image Thy faithful, who are themselves also taken up into the sublimity of Thine oblation, *de tuis donis ac datis*.[1]

August Victim, Lord Jesus, it seems to me I hold Thee in my arms when I extend them now, supplicating the Father to look with a propitious and serene countenance upon Thy Sacrifice, this Sacrifice of Thy blessed Passion, *beatae Passionis*, here commemorated, enacted, applied; the Sacrifice which Thy *Resurrection* consecrated, placing thereon, as it were, the seal of God Who accepted it; the Sacrifice which Thy *glorious Ascension* elevated even into the glory of the saints in order to let it bear witness there eternally in the presence of God for us.[2]

O divine Victim, Thou art Purity itself, *Hostiam puram!*[3] From the beginning of the world, no other victim, however faithfully offered, has been able to appear in this Presence without at least the appearance of some stain.

Thou art *Holiness* itself, *Hostiam sanctam*,[4] and Thou bestowest holiness. Until now none was able to wash away the sins of the world; no other had the power to cleanse with blood the human conscience and separate it from all Things in order to give it into the power of God alone.

---

1 Of Thine own gifts bestowed upon us.
2 Hebr. 9: 24.   3 A pure Victim.   4 A holy Victim.

Thou art immaculate, *Hostiam immaculatam!*[5] Thine innocence is that of God Himself. When the Father looks upon it, He sees therein His own reflection and with fullness of love takes pleasure in this innocence which mirrors His own eternal Beauty.

I hail Thee, holy Bread of eternal Life! Thou hast ascended to Heaven, where Thou remainest the food of Angels. There Thou preparest for us the feast that will satisfy our longing. O Bread of God, make me a host, holy like Thee, immaculate like Thee, pure like Thee!

I hail Thee, *Chalice of everlasting salvation!* I await with an impatience which Thou knowest, that moment forever blessed when Thou shalt still the thirst of my soul in the Blood which inebriates Thine elect. Wound in the side of Jesus, Thou art this glorious Chalice sparkling with inner fires which in Heaven delights Thy priests found faithful to Thee. Oh, lead me to Thy Fountain, Thou Saviour of the world, Thou Friend of the priests who were victims with Thee, Thou immaculate Victim!

---

[5] A spotless Victim.

XLIX

DIGNERIS ET ACCEPTA HABERE

DO THOU VOUCHSAFE TO ACCEPT

Most merciful Father, Thy holy Victim, Thy pure and immaculate Victim, possesses in Himself every right to be graciously accepted by Thee; is not this *Thy Beloved Son in Whom Thou art well pleased?*[1]

Yet I plead, O Father Who lovest me. Thou wast pleased to accept the sacrifice of Thy child Abel, whose *justice*, celebrated in Holy Scripture, was so clear and beautiful a symbol of eternal Justice, of Jesus, Thy Well-Beloved! Well, then, here is that very Justice: yes, here is the sacred Victim *immolated* by the sinner's injustice, here, in my hands, which the Church by her consecration has been pleased to make *holy and venerable*. O Father, look upon this Victim, I beseech Thee, with Thy look of peace, the fruit of which will nourish my soul!

Thou didst receive graciously the offering of *Abraham our Patriarch*, who without hesitation delivered up to Thee Isaac, the son of the promise, bone of his bone, flesh of his flesh, in whom were placed all the hopes of the human race. Thou didst wonder at his faith and obedience, at his complete abandonment to Thy will: *and it was reputed to him unto justice.*[2]

Here, then, in my holy and venerable hands, I offer unto Thee the *Only-begotten Son Who is in Thy Bosom,*[3] the *Son of Thine eternal dilection,*[4] Him Whom *Thy too great love* did not hesitate to deliver into the hands of executioners to be nailed to the Cross, in order that this Saviour should thus *draw all things to Himself*[5] and, through Himself, to Thee! Oh, let Thine eyes rest on Him now with the same look of loving-kindness with which Thou enfoldedst Him when He cried out to Thee: "Father, into Thy hands I commend My spirit!"[6]

It was thus Thou didst look upon the *sacrifice of Melchisedech*, Thy

---

1 Matt. 3: 17.   2 Gen. 15: 6.   3 John 1: 18.
4 Col. 1: 13.   5 John 12: 32. 6 Luke 23: 46.

High Priest, the *Priest of the Most High*. He offered unto Thee the bread and the wine;[7] and Thy Heart, O Father, was moved. Thou sawest afar, in the ages to come, *the holy Bread of eternal Life and the Chalice of everlasting salvation* which the *eternal Priest* would offer unto Thee *after the manner of this same Melchisedech,* who prefigures mysteriously Thy Best-beloved Melchisedech *without father, without mother, without genealogy, King of Peace, having neither beginning of days nor end of life, but Who, likened unto the Son of God, continueth a priest forever.*[8] Behold this Bread and this Chalice: I lift them up toward Thee, O Father of this eternal Priest, and I beseech Thee to vouchsafe to receive them, to look upon these offerings propitiously, with the fatherly regard which is at once reassuring, winning, and enticing.

Lo, here before the eyes of Thy divine mercy, is *the Holy Sacrifice*, the one which, infinitely more than those of Abel, Abraham, and Melchisedech, which after all were but pale symbols of this sublime reality, has the power to please Thee, has the power to sanctify and render immaculate, like this divine Victim, the soul that approaches Thee to offer Him confidently unto Thee.

O Holy Sacrifice, immaculate Host, I look upon Thee also, my human gaze absorbed in the gaze of my God! I love Thee, I give Thee all my faith, all my hope, all my love. Sanctify me, purify me, and clothe my soul in the beauty pleasing to our Heavenly Father.

---

7 Gen. 14: 18.   8 Heb. 7: 2 *ff.*

L

JUBE HAEC PERFERRI

COMMAND THAT THESE THINGS BE BORNE

Supplices te rogamus. We must humbly beseech Thee, Almighty God, to command that these things be borne by the hands of Thy holy Angel to Thine altar on high, in the sight of Thy divine Majesty! Mysterious, almost incomprehensible prayer! Who will tell its height and its depth, its length and its breadth? It has the dimensions of Thy love, Lord Jesus;[1] need one say more?

Supplices. I bow down low, my hands pressed upon the altar, with which I seem to have become one. The altar is Thine own symbol, O Christ, the symbol of Thy sacred Humanity, whereon flowed, and ever flows, that Most Precious Blood which refreshes my soul.

I bow down and I supplicate: my supplication is this prayer forged in the Fire of the Holy, Trinity, in the love which eternally unites the Father and the Son. In it one feels a divine Flame that burns the priest who utters it, as it burned Mary, Queen and Mother of priests, of Apostles, on the day of Pentecost.

Father, almighty Father, grant that my hands, holy and venerable in Thy Christ, may take up from this altar the pure, holy, and immaculate Victim, the Host more pleasing in Thine eyes than the sacrifice of Abel the just, of Abraham our Patriarch, or of Thy priest Melchisedech; grant that I may lift It up to Thy heavenly Altar in the sight of Thy Majesty.

The Altar, I repeat, was and is the sacred Humanity of Thy Son, Who was at once Victim, Priest, and Altar of His Sacrifice; but this Altar has become sublime; that is, it was raised higher than the Heavens which it penetrated, when Thou, O Father, having vouchsafed to accept this Sacrifice of Calvary here reenacted and commemorated in the Mass, didst decree that it should be consummated in eternity.

1 Eph. 3: 18–19.

At the Resurrection, at the Ascension of this Priest, the Unique Priest of Thy glory, Thou didst deign to seal with the kiss of final reconciliation the Work of Redemption by the Cross. Then did Heaven and earth greet the triumphal entrance of the Conqueror of death into a Temple greater even than the Gift of His Humanity to His elect, into the Temple of Thy Glory, that is, into Thy Bosom, the *Bosom of the Father in which is the Only-begotten Son;*[2] then didst Thou have This God-Man to sit at Thy Right Hand, sharing with Him eternally Thy Power and this same Glory. This present Sacrifice offered unto Thee re-enacts this glorious mystery; for in high Heaven, in the Bosom of Thy Glory, Jesus remains the perpetual Victim, *Hostia perpetua:* Thus He crowns and consummates His ministry, and the power of the Sacrifice of the Cross endures forever. O Mystery!

Ah, certainly, all was accomplished, all was merited on the Cross, and all is applied here on this earthly altar; yet in Heaven, O Jesus, Thou placest as it were a seal upon Thy character of Mediator and supreme Pontiff. Thy blessed Passion, Thy glorious Resurrection, Thy wondrous Ascension constitute, in fact, but a single mystery, the mystery of Thy Priesthood. In Heaven Thou enjoyest its power and from on high, still bending down over Thy Church, Thou scatterest over her the riches of its redemptive treasure. That the earthly altar is so effective is because it is as if welded, so to speak, to that of Heaven, that is, to the holy Humanity of the Word.

Unlike the High Priest of the Law who dared enter only once each year, and that trembling, into the Holy of Holies,[3] Thou, hast entered in forever *even within the veil,* where Thy Father is revealed to Thee, *usque ad interiora velaminis;*[4] nor dost Thou enter with the blood of calves, but with Thine own Blood.[5] Thou appearest now before the Face of this august Father, and for us, *ut appareat nunc vultui Dei pro nobis.*[6] Thou appearest before Him covered with Thy glorious wounds, which like flaming suns illumine the City of God. Through them the voice of Thy Priesthood speaks for us, Thy members, left in the valley of tears; for Thou art there only to intercede for us, *semper vivens ad interpellandum pro nobis.*[7]

Thou dost still more: Thou, the Minister, the Liturgist of the Holies,

---

[2] John 1: 18.   [3] Heb. 9: 7.   [4] *Ibid.* 6: 19.   [5] *Ibid.* 9: 12.
[6] That He may appear now in the presence of God for us (Heb. 9: 24).
[7] Always living to make intercession for us (Heb. 7: 25).

Sanctorum minister,[8] bringest us into Thy Glory, the Glory of Thy Father. Every soul, to ascend into this Glory, must pass through Thy hands, in order to become therein a perpetual Victim, with Thee, and so be presented to the Heavenly Father.

Not only dost Thou guide the soul into this Glory; Thou sustainest it there, giving it to drink of the fountains of living waters, to which Thou leadest it, O Lamb of God, that there it may satisfy its thirst for love. *Agnus reget eos et deducet eos ad vitae fontes aquarum.*[9]

Finally, Thou offerest Thyself there constantly to Thy Father and, so offering Thyself forever, Thou receivest us into Thine oblation, that we may be an eternal gift to God, a victim of oblation, *oblationis hostiam: et per eam nosmetipsos tibi perfice munus aeternum.*[10]

Today Thou hearest us, then, Lord Jesus, to that sublime Altar which Thou art. Yes, this Victim of oblation is immersed in Thy Glory, O Father, by which fact He proclaims unceasingly through the centuries Thy divine acceptance of Him. And while, in the Holy Mass, He prolongs His oblation, He receives constantly on high, in and through this Glory, the indisputable pledge of Thy satisfaction. There Thou offerest forever to Thy Father, O divine Victim, the adoration and the thanksgiving of Thy holy Humanity; Thou offerest the adoration and thanksgiving of Mary, Thy Mother and ours, of the souls of the Blessed, Thy Mystic Body; and this offering Thou makest in the state of resurrection and glory, Thine and ours, which is the confirmation and consequence of Thy triumphant Sacrifice, by which, on the Cross, Thou conquerest Satan, and sin, and death. *Tu nobis Victor, Rex....*[11]

O Michael, Angel of God, Prince of the celestial hosts, and thou, Gabriel, Power of God, herald of the mysteries of Jesus, thou also, my Holy Guardian Angel who wouldst never abandon me, especially in this solemn moment, and thou, holy Angel who offerest the prayers of all the saints, of Heaven, of purgatory and of earth,[12] do ye accompany the priestly offering of the Angel of the Father, Jesus, my Saviour: it is the offering both of Je-

---

8 Heb. 8: 2.
9 For the Lamb ... shall rule them and shall lead them to the fountains of the waters of life (Apoc. 7: 17).
10 And through it make of us, too, an eternal offering to Thee (*Secret* of the Mass of Trinity Sunday).
11 Do Thou, victor King, have mercy on us (*Paschal Sequence*).   12 Apoc. 8: 3–5.

sus and the Church, of the Head and of the members, of the total Christ: the Father calls us, that He may rejoice in this homage which confesses all His rights over the Mystic Body of Jesus the Well-Beloved.

Then, satisfied with our faith and our love, He bends toward us *with every heavenly blessing and grace*. Through this Body and Blood which we offer unto Him, He sees us merged in His Son; and He comes to us to fill us with His fullness, *to fill us unto all the fullness of God*.[13] Amen.

---

13 Eph. 3: 19.

LI

IN CHRISTO QUIESCENTIBUS

TO ALL THAT REST IN CHRIST

The gaze of the priest of Jesus and of all who are participating actively in the Sacrifice, in the oblation of the holy and immaculate Victim, is rapt in the Holy of Holies and is fixed as by a sort of enchantment in a prayer which would seem to be rather of Heaven than of earth. "There can be no higher form of contemplation than the Holy Mass," says St Vincent Ferrer.

The work of life has operated in me. Dead to all things since sharing in the immolation of my Master, I have become an altar bread which the immaculate Lamb of God invests with His Sanctity, with His purity and virtue. By the *Supplices* I was as if transported to Heaven, there to become with Christ an *odor of sweetness* glorifying the Trinity of the Father, of the Son, and of the Holy Spirit.

Already the Church Militant is one with me in this flight of grace, while the Church of Heaven is present at this species of assumption by which I am torn away from the earth. Now these bounteous gifts, marks of favor from the Lord to my soul and the souls of all present about the altar, have still to be shared by the Church of purgatory.

These suffering souls, so dear to God, these souls for whom this Precious Blood is flowing, for whom it is flowing, one might say, upon the sublime Altar in the presence of the divine Majesty, these souls are panting for God; and unable to do anything for themselves, they now, by the ministry of the priest who makes official intercession for them, lift their arms in that hieratic gesture which is a supplication for mercy.

What glory reverts to the Heavenly Father when but a single one of these souls enters at last into *the place of refreshment, light, and peace!* What joy floods the Sacred Humanity of the Son! What streams of glowing love flow from the Holy Spirit to this chosen soul being made molten in this brazier of God's ineffable operations! And what fathomless consolation and delight must be the part of this soul, of this member of the Christ, which has attained the supreme goal and enters with an eternal certitude into the Body of the Church of Jesus, here forever united with her Head!

To realize this marvel, to obtain so great a glory for the Holy Trinity, to give so perfect a consolation to such a soul, to one whose unsatisfied love is battering at the gates of a Heaven which still repulses it—for so much of God's glory is inherent in His justice!—ah! what would one not do to gain this end? Even though it were necessary to hear thousands of Masses! Would that be too great a price for opening to this servant of God the sacred wound which will confer upon Him eternal blessedness?

O most kind Lord, most merciful Father, to all *Thy servants and handmaids who are gone before us with the sign of faith,* the holy faith which enabled them to live for Heaven; to all who *sleep in the sleep of peace* and the embrace of Thy grace; *to these, O Lord, and to all that rest in Christ,* Thy Well-beloved, to all that have been made Thy beloved in Him, *grant, we beseech Thee,* I and all Thy Church, *a place of refreshment, light, and peace!*

LII

NOBIS QUOQUE PECCATORIBUS

TO US SINNERS ALSO

Before the most holy Altar of Heaven the saints of God are exulting; the souls of purgatory arrive in that place of divine refreshment, transported thither by the imploring cries of the praying Church; and we also, we poor sinners, sigh for this fatherland, the bourne of our hope, this country *where neither mourning, nor crying, nor sorrow shall be any more.*[1] Take pity on us, O Lord, on us poor sinners, whose hearts long for Thee!

O Father, I long to be with Thee and to that end I place my hope in the *multitude of Thy mercies.* The grace above all grace, is the final grace, in view of which especially Thou madest me a Christian, madest me a priest. It is the grace toward which tends the whole astonishing series of these tender mercies with which Thou fillest our lives, O God our Salvation, Whose desire is that we come to Thee!

Come, Lord, come Thou to me also through Jesus Christ! Thou earnest to all Thy saints, men and women, to all those whom Thy Church desires me at this point in the Sacrifice to recall to Thy Heart of goodness, to Thy Father-Heart which loves me, that they may be for me intercessors and friends who will lead me to Thee.

I call then to my aid Thine Apostles, Thy martyrs, Thine illustrious virgins. Among these saints I recognize Thy Prophet, *greatest among those that are born of women,*[2] him who pointed to the Lamb, Thy Lamb, O God, the Victim, the Host of this very Sacrifice. Oh, may this martyr, this witness for the pure in heart, open Thy Heaven one day for me and unite me with Jesus Christ, Thy Best-Beloved!

I salute among them also Stephen the deacon, who, while still on earth in the midst of his combat, saw the Heavens open and looked upon the glory

---

[1] Apoc. 21: 4.   [2] Luke 7: 28.

of this Thy Christ, crying out: "Behold, I see the Son of Man standing on the right hand of God!"[3] O St Stephen, bring us, bring me into this glory!

And you, holy widows, Saints Felicitas and Perpetua, and you wondrous virgins, the richest of the pure gems of Holy Church, Agatha, Lucy, Agnes, Cecilia, whose life and death were one deep longing for God and His Christ, intercede for us, for me, that where ye are, we may one day be with you, beatified in this Light of Light which suffuses you, filling you with its plenitude.

Nobis quoque peccatoribus. We strike our breasts, we sinners, unworthy on every count to appear at last before this divine Majesty Whose delight is in the incomparable Beauty of the sublime Altar whereon a God is immolated. *O Lord, consider not our merits;* they are nothing; but grant us, from the superabundance of Thy mercy, *Thine own free pardon;* for by this pardon dost Thou not make Thine omnipotence most clearly manifest?

Grant us, O Father, grant me the hope of joining the company of Thine elect! Let the desire of Heaven appear constantly before my spirit and inflame my heart. Let me die to all other ambition: let my life be directed once and for all toward the supreme Reality wherein lies my salvation, O God Who lovest me!

---

3 Acts 7: 55.

LIII

PER QUEM HAEC OMNIA BONA CREAS

THROUGH WHOM THOU CREATEST ALL THESE GIFTS

To the very end of this Holy Sacrifice, the treatment of the immaculate Host answers all the conditions of an offering which is a Sacrament, that is, an outward sign. The appearances of the Bread and the Wine constitute this visible sign. There is, to be sure, no longer any bread nor any wine, but their appearances remain, hiding beneath them the real substance of Jesus Christ, the Lamb of God.

This Host, this sublime creation, is the *Gift* of the Father, of the Son, of the Holy Ghost. It is the *Gift* of man who gives it back to God. It is a Gift which, together with the innumerable hosts which we are in union with Jesus, constitutes the *Treasures* of God, *haec omnia bona*. Ah, what a creation is this Sacrifice, employing as it does such a Sacrament!

The Bread and the Wine, now, by transubstantiation, the Body and Blood of Jesus, truly have the appearance of the first fruits of all God's creation, since they served, and still serve, under their appearances, the ministry of the universal Victim of the Holy Trinity, the Only-begotten Son of the Father.

Per quem haec omnia, semper bona creas.[1] It is, in fact, through Thee, Lord Jesus, Mediator between God and man, it is through Thee and by Thy power that Thou createst all these gifts which compose the totality of the Sacrifice of our altars, that is, Thee, all of us, and myself, Thy minister.

Creas. Thus Thou recreatest me and restorest me to my first and essential destiny, the glory of God: this recreation, begun at Baptism, Thou didst desire only in order to prepare me for Thy Sacrifice and for the worship of which it is the center. So wouldst Thou have me to be victim with Thee, Who art the holy Victim of the Father.

---

[1] The English version of the Latin in this Meditation, from the *Nobis quoque peccatoribus*, reads: Through Whom, O Lord, Thou dost create, hallow, quicken, and bless these Thine ever-bountiful gifts and give them to us.

Sanctificas. Here, therefore, I find *the fount of all my holiness.*[2] A saint is one *separated*, one "set apart" to belong to God alone. At the altar I am consumed by the Fire which is Thy Holy Spirit, in the Fire which purifies me, tears me away from the earth, and bears me upward into Thy Light, into union with Thee.

Vivificas. Here Thou quickenest me, leadest me into free participation in Thy Life, the Life Thou drawest forth from the Bosom of This Trinity whence Thou *camest to visit the earth and to inebriate it; visitasti terram et inebriasti eam.*[3]

Benedicis. This is the divine benediction which will one day make of me, which is one day to make of me—this is my hope and my tearful prayer—which is one day to make of me one of the *Blessed of the Father;*[4] blessed because found *conformable to Thine image*, O Jesus, His *First-born amongst many brethren.*[5]

Et praestas nobis. Thus to be *Victim* with Thee, through Thee, in Thee, Lord Jesus, is the source of all the other benefits, spiritual and temporal, which have come, and which continue to come to us, by the sublime channel of the Holy Mass.

O powerful Redemption! Thou renewest all things; thou renewest even myself!

---

2 *Secret* of the Mass of St Ignatius of Loyola.
3 Ps. 64: 10.   4 Matt. 25: 34.   5 Rom. 8: 29.

LIV

OMNIS HONOR ET GLORIA

ALL HONOR AND GLORY

This is the point of culmination in the rite of Oblation. Together the Body and the Blood of Jesus Christ are uplifted toward the Almighty Father, thus indicating the unity of the wondrous Sacrament, of which the priest of the Church and the assembled faithful are about to partake. A last time the sacred liturgy signalizes this by this elevation. Showing us this immaculate Victim, this *holy Bread of eternal Life* and this *Chalice of everlasting Salvation*, it seems to cry out to us: "*Sancta Sanctis*, behold the Holy of Holies destined for the holy!"

Omnis honor et gloria. To Thee, O Father, Father Almighty, Creator of worlds visible and invisible, to Thee all honor and glory! To Thee my adorations, to Thee my thanksgivings, to Thee my supplications, to Thee my expiations! All this is Thy honor and Thy glory; all this honors Thee in the sight of Thy creatures; all this glorifies Thee amid the shining glory of the saints.

In substance the Holy Mass has been celebrated; the Work of the Redemption has been renewed; all the saints of Heaven have bent down over the Lamb of God and have been decked in new splendor in the presence of the Precious Blood, which is their exultation and the cause of their beatitude. The souls of purgatory have been refreshed in this saving Stream of the Precious Blood, which diminishes their sufferings and at last delivers them. The Church Militant has just obtained from this Precious Blood measureless pardon and incalculable graces. All this contributes to the *honor and glory* of the Father.

All this is the operation of Love, the work of the Holy Ghost, through Whom Jesus Christ has offered Himself to the honor and the glory of His Father: a work of love, wherefrom shine forth all the tender mercies which today again, *have just descended from the boundless ocean* of the Holy Trinity *to visit man; visitasti nos oriens ex alto,*[1] and ravish him away to God: *In unitate Spiritus Sancti.*[2]

Per Ipsum.[3] Yes, O Father Who lovest us, it is through Jesus, Thy Priest, Thy Victim, Thine Altar, that the Oblation of Thy Church is raised on high, immaculate and victorious. This Oblation has irresistible force, *being heard for the reverence* with which Thou envelopest it.[4]

Cum Ipso.[5] O Father, Thy children cleave to this Priest, this Victim, this Altar, to Jesus Christ. Not for a moment do they allow themselves to be separated from Him or His strength, from the power of His prayer, for they would fain ascend *with Him to Thy Most Holy Altar* into the presence of Thy Majesty.

In Ipso.[6] They long to abide, *they do abide, in Him always that their prayer may be heard*[7] and their desires granted beyond the utmost measure of their hopes. The effect of this Oblation is to seal their deep union with a God Who adores, thanks, supplicates, and appeases a God.

Omnis honor et gloria. This, Lord, is all the honor and glory Thou claimest from Thy faithful; Oh, do Thou accept our Oblation! Vouchsafe to look kindly upon it in the Name of Him through Whom, with Whom, and in Whom we obtain access to Thee, now and always, world without end, *per omnia saecula saeculorum. Amen.* Ah, yes! May it so be forever and forever! *Amen.*

---

1 The Orient from on high hath visited us (Luke 1: 78).
2 In the unity of the Holy Ghost.   3 Through Him.
4 Heb. 5: 7.   5 With Him.   6 In Him.   7 John 15: 7.

COMMUNION IN THE SACRIFICE

From the Our Father to the End of the Mass

DETACHMENT, DEATH TO SELF, HAVE MADE THE SOUL A HOST OF SACRIFICE WHICH GOD IS PLEASED TO ACCEPT; THEREFORE HE INVITES IN TO AN INTIMATE COMMUNION. THIS WILL BE HIS OWN BANQUET AND ALSO THAT OF THE SOUL WHICH HAS REACHED THE GOAL OF ITS DESIRES: IT KNOWS HENCEFORTH THE FULLNESS OF LOVE.

LV

PATER NOSTER

OUR FATHER

The Hour of Supper[1] has almost arrived, when the Bread of God will be distributed, and the Wine of Life poured. I must become one with the sublime Sacrifice I have just offered. So shall I *be found in Jesus Christ*[2] and be more nearly—as nearly as one can hope to be here on earth—Priest, Victim, and Altar of His Oblation. Ever higher and farther the Mystery rises; it is going to plunge me into God: infallibly it is leading me *into the Bosom of the Father where dwells the Only-Begotten Son.*[3]

Our Father, Who art in Heaven! Yes, what a mystery of love! In the form of a wondrous Sacrament our Sacrifice is offered, in order that we may be filled with the *holy Bread of eternal Life* and quench our thirst from the *Chalice of everlasting salvation.* This mystery, I repeat, is a mystery of love: it is the crown and apex of all Thy graces today. Ah, true it is, *most merciful Father,* that Thou lovest us too much, *propter nimiam caritatem suam.*[4] But, the fact is, Thou seest us now only in Thy perpetual Victim, Whom, now that Thou hast been pleased to accept Him, having, as it were, consumed Him in the fire of Thy Spirit of Love, it is Thy sole desire to give to us as food and drink for the Life eternal.

Father, our Father! And when Thou hast strengthened us with this Manna, when Thou hast infused us, in a sense, into Jesus Christ, then Thou wilt unite us to each other through this Sacrament of Christian Unity. Yes, Thou wilt be *Our Father,* and we shall go to Thee thenceforth only in this Unity, "the greatest of all possessions."[5] In this Unity which consummates us in Thee, we shall be completely restored to the Blessed Trinity of Father, Son, and Holy Spirit; the Work of the Redemption will really be renewed and increased in our souls; we shall live from God. We shall be in Jesus

---

[1] Luke 14: 17.   [2] Phil. 3: 9.   [3] John 1: 18.   [4] Eph. 2: 4.
[5] St Ignatius of Antioch to the Ephesians.

Christ, and Thou shalt say again of Him, Thou shalt say of us hidden in Him: "This is My Beloved Son, in Whom I am well pleased."[6]

Father, our Father, Who art in Heaven. It is for Thee, for Thy grace, to prepare us for this feast of love, for this banquet at which Thou pourest into our hearts this inebriating wine, the Precious Blood of the Spotless Lamb.

Therefore, Thy Son Jesus, *the Son of Thy Love,*[7] having taught us how to pray to Thee, we make bold to cry out to Thee: *Our Father!* Lord God, open our lips, sanctify our bodies and our souls, purify our minds, in order that we may cry out to Thee as true suppliants and in all humility and confidence: *Our Father, Who art in Heaven!*

Father, Father! Ah, how sweet is God's Name! It moves my inmost being; it expands my soul, lifts it on pinions of hope, even makes it audacious. *Father!* What may not the little child expect from a Father, from a Father Who is God, when it cries out to Thee: *Our Father, Who art in Heaven!* Our Father, Who art in the fiery Heaven of Thy Trinity, in the merciful Heaven of the sacred Humanity of Thy Well-Beloved, in the most pure Heaven of the Immaculate Virgin Mother, in the luminous Heaven of Thy Seraphim and Cherubim and all Thy Angels, in the wondrous Heaven of Thy saints, Thy saints of paradise, purgatory and earth! *Our Father,* Who art Father in all the Heavens which sing Thy praise, have pity on us, on me! Give us, give me Jesus Christ!

---

6 Matt. 3: 17.   7 Col. 1: 13.

LVI

SANCTIFICETUR NOMEN TUUM

HALLOWED BE THY NAME

O Father, Who art in Heaven, the desire which above all others must occupy my soul at this hour of the divine banquet is to hallow Thy Name. Yes, it is for that first of all that I am going to partake of the Body and Blood of Jesus Christ: *Father! Hallowed be Thy Name!*

Thy Name is God, for Thou art the Name we give Thee. God and His Name are one, and this One is All. O most holy Name, I adore Thee; I adore in Thee all the infinite perfections of God, which are in the very essence of this Name: Power, Wisdom, Goodness, Justice, Mercy, Immensity, Eternity, and Glory forever and ever! I adore Thee, I sink humbly before Thee, I, who am nothing, before Thee Who art All!

Thy Person is God, *O God;* yet we call Thee also *Father, our Father!* Of all the revelations of Thee made to us by Thy Well-beloved Son, the eternal Object of Thy good pleasure, this Name is perhaps the most profound. Thou callest Thyself Father; my Baptism has made me Thy child after the likeness of Thy First-Born; and my faith tells me that all my sanctity must consist in letting myself be more and more completely possessed by the Spirit of Thy Son Which was poured into my soul in that moment of regeneration in order that He might lift this soul up to Thee and cry out therein: *Father, Father!* [1]

Then *hallowed be Thy Name* of God and Father! But what am I saying? Is not Thy very Name Thy Sanctity? How, then, can my nothingness be of use in sanctifying it? What can I add to something that is already infinitely Holy?

Certainly the very essence of Thy Name is Sanctity; but is it not susceptible nevertheless of a sanctification—extrinsic, to be sure—which it

---

[1] Gal. 4: 6.

does not yet have, will not have so long as we, O Father, Thy creatures, but especially we Thy children, do not seek above all things else Thy glory, Thy glory alone, committing ourselves entirely to Thee, depending upon Thee with all that we are and all that we have, with our whole mind and heart, with all the gifts with which Thou hast laden us, as well in the order of nature as in the order of grace?

O God and Father, hallowed be Thy Name! This Name of God and Father will be hallowed by me if, I, passionately seeking Thy glory, become as a little child in my search, if I attain more and more perfectly to this attitude of simplicity, of confidence, of absolute abandonment to Thy Fatherhood over me, whom Thou hast made a *member*[2] of Thy Well-beloved Son, me Thine heir and His joint-heir[3] in the glory to come.

Hallowed be Thy Name, O Father! That will be the first cry of Jesus Christ from my soul unto Thee in a moment when He will so humble Himself as to become my food and my drink.

And shall this not be thy first thought, O my soul, when thou receivest the Body and Blood of Thy Christ?

---

2 1 Cor. 6: 15.   3 Rom. 8: 17.

LVII

ADVENIAT REGNUM TUUM

THY KINGDOM COME

I can neither really desire nor seek this glory of my Heavenly Father excepting in Jesus Christ, my Priest, my Victim, and my Altar; I can seek it only in Him, through Whom, with Whom, and in Whom are rendered to the Lord all honor and glory.

This, then, is the great work of my sanctification: to enter into Jesus Christ, to pass from the human into the divine, from the old man into the new man, from Adam into Jesus; this transition will be my Pasch which, in sum, will free me from the bondage of Satan to deliver me unto the reign of my Saviour within me. *Adveniat regnum tuum.* Father, Thy kingdom come!

Thy Kingdom come, O Father, Who art in Heaven! Does not the Communion I am about to receive in the Body and Blood of Jesus Thy Best-Beloved have in view this very end and consummation? Now my soul, delivered from its sins in the cleansing state of compunction, and flooded, in the state of illumination, with the splendors of the Word, has still to learn by personal experience the unspeakable delights of the unitive life: the anticipated reign of Jesus Christ within me.

Thy Kingdom come! Come, Lord Jesus, *King of kings and Lord of lords;*[1] make Thy solemn entrance today into my heart; reign Thou in my innermost being. Is not that Thy true kingdom?[2] And then act upon all my forces, the forces of my soul, of my mind, of my heart, upon the energies of my body; reign Thou absolutely; I give over to Thee straightway all the powers and possessions of my being; do Thou but reign over me and all that belongs to me.

Yet what have I, Lord, but my nothingness, my weakness, the sad results of my sins? Nevertheless, reign even over all that, in order that I may

---

1 Apoc. 19: 16.   2 Luke 17: 21.

pass into Thee, in order that Thou once more with great desire, mayest eat Thy Pasch with me.³

Then shall I pass and enter into sincere, lasting,⁴ and sweet communion with Thee in Thy functions as Priest, Victim, and Altar of Thy Sacrifice. Then wilt Thou take possession of my being; Thou wilt offer it in truth, in untold plenitude to my Father Who is in Heaven.

Yes, my soul will be filled with Thee, Lord Jesus. Made the city of Thy reign, it will have from that time forth but one passion, a passion essential to Thy saints: namely, to extend the reign of my Heavenly Father, this reign which is Thy very Self, O my Christ! I shall burn with the desire to make Thee known and loved; to lead all souls, sinners especially, to Thy sacred feet, that there they may be bound fast with faith and love and, casting themselves into Thine arms, may still their longing, even as I, at the wound of love where Thou refreshest all who thirst for the Life eternal which Thou art!

O Father, may Thy Kingdom come! May the reign of Jesus Christ begin! *For He must reign oportet autem Illum regnare.*⁵

---

3 Luke 22: 15.   4 See last paragraph, page 186.   5 Cor. 15: 25.

LVIII

FIAT VOLUNTAS TUA

THY WILL BE DONE

Our Father Who art in Heaven, Thy will be done on earth as it is in Heaven! This is the price of Thy glory, Thy Kingdom demands it: O Will, O Love, O Spirit of the Father and of the Son!

Thy Will, Father is Love. When I pray *that Thy will be fulfilled on earth as it is in Heaven,* I am imploring Thee to raise my soul and all its powers to the height of Thy divine Love, to admit it to the ineffable communion of that eternal Embrace which is Thy Holy Spirit, that substantial Kiss of Father and Son, Their eternal Bond and the adorable End—without end—of the vital operations of the Holy Trinity.

In a little while, O Jesus, I shall receive Thy Body and Thy Blood; and Thou wilt transport me into God, into His Will, into His Love; Thou wilt let me enjoy this Kiss, the delight of Thy Holiness, the delight of all Thine angels and Thy saints.

How would it be possible for me not to desire today all that Thou desirest of me? What is Thy will for me today? I know and I do not know. When I see in the light of Thy holy Law all that Thou hast Thyself imposed upon me, my duty, my work, my charge of souls, then I know, O my God, what Thy will is.

But the rest I know not: sufferings, troubles, renunciations, sacrifices, oblations of all kinds, the total loss of myself and all I love. Thou canst demand everything: *Thy will be done, O Father, on earth as it is in Heaven.*

I desire to accomplish Thy will in this Christ with Whose Flesh and Blood Thou unitest my being today in Holy Communion, that so I may *do all things in the Name of Our Lord Jesus Christ, giving thanks to Thee by Him in all things.*[1]

---

1 Col. 3: 17.

I desire to do *Thy will on earth as in Heaven*, in Thy presence, ceasing not, the while I fulfill it, to keep my soul's gaze fixed serenely upon Thee, my God, as the saints whom Thou hast admitted to the beatific Vision find the steadfastness of love in that absorption which gives them wholly into Thy power.

I desire the fulfillment of Thy will, Father, in all my brothers as well as in myself; I desire it in joy and in sorrow, in wealth and in poverty, on the Cross as well as in the glory to come. It is my good, it is my strength, and it remains forever my victory; for whoever does Thy will, my God, Thou wilt do his.

Our Father, Who art in Heaven, hallowed be Thy Name in glory: *Thy kingdom come* through Christ: *Thy will be done* in the Holy Spirit. This is the most beautiful fruit of my Communion now so close at hand. It is a fruit of divine love, of that love which will enkindle a fire in the depths of my being and consume my soul before Thee as a living and holy oblation. *Fiat.*

LIX

PANEM NOSTRUM QUOTIDIANUM DA NOBIS

GIVE US OUR DAILY BREAD

Father, our Father, Who art in Heaven, we are Thy children, *we are the little ones who ask for bread:*[1] and Thy Bread is Jesus Christ. By accepting His Sacrifice, by receiving this Victim, *pure, holy,* and *spotless* as He is in Thine eyes, Thou hast in some sort made Him Thy very own Bread, O Father; and Thou admittest us to this sacred banquet with but a single desire: to give us also to eat of this holy Bread. *Give us this day our daily Bread.*

I hunger for Thee, O Jesus Christ, for Thee, Priest, Victim, Altar of my Sacrifice! And to think that in a moment, if Thou deign to come to me—and Thou dost urgently desire to come!—I shall be filled with this Bread which Thou art, the Bread *that came down from Heaven giving Life to the world,*[2] giving life to my soul. It gives life even to my body in the sense that, by a mysterious and sanctifying action, It impels it forward in the way that leads to the resurrection and the Life eternal.[3]

Bread of God, I am the wayside beggar crying out to Thee in my misery: *Jesus, Son of David, have mercy on me!*[4] Let me not fall from exhaustion on the rough and weary road that leads to God!

True Bread![5] Come to me who hunger for Thy Truth! I long to know Thee, O Jesus Christ, I long to penetrate farther and farther into Thy *mystery of godliness,*[6] to explore the dimensions of Thine infinite charity, its depth which engulfs my nothingness, its height which towers into the sublimity of the Most High, its breadth which spreads its treasures before me, its length[7] which has pursued me from eternity.

---

1 Lam. 4: 4.   2 John 6: 59.   3 *Ibid.*   4 Mark 10: 47.
5 *Lauda Sion.*   6 1 Tim. 3: 16.   7 Ephes. 3: 17–18.

Bread of children,[8] of God's children, Thou comest to me to nourish my supernatural being, which Thy Father desires to see grow more and more closely conformable to Thine own image, Thine own beauty, Thine own sanctity, and which He desires to make more and more truly Thy brother, *O First-born amongst many brethren*[9] of our Father Who is in Heaven!

Come, oh, come *this day!* Yes, do Thou come every day of my life; for Thou art indispensable to that soul whose remedy Thou hast become for all sin and imperfection, for everything that might, even in the slightest degree, displease Thy heavenly Father.

Come, *holy Bread of eternal Life,* food which is a foretaste of the homeland of Heaven. Come, Bread of the Father, That givest complete detachment from every creature, That freest me from the bewitching of earthly vanity,[10] to set my heart aflame with the desire for realities as yet invisible, for the joys with which Thou wilt fill me in the Beatific Vision above.

Come, Bread of Angels, Bread of Seraphim and Cherubim, who contemplate Thee in the inconceivable outpouring of eternally enravished love!

Father, give us this day our daily Bread, yes, ours, the Bread Which creates, guards, strengthens our brotherly unity, our unity as Christians, who, *being many, are one bread, one body, all partaking of one bread.*[11]

---

8 *Lauda Sion.*   9 Rom. 8: 29.   10 Wis. 4: 12.   11 1 Cor. 10: 17.

LX

ET DIMITTE NOBIS SICUT ET NOS

AND FORGIVE US AS WE FORGIVE

There is but one disposition of soul truly fundamental for the reception of Thy Body and Blood, Lord Jesus: that is charity. Before we may approach Thee, we have need of Thy divine love, that is to say, of Thine unspeakable mercy, of Thy loving-kindness, O Bread of God, Bread of Our Father! But only in such measure as our hearts incline unto our neighbor in love and forgiveness and all kindness will this mercifulness be manifested to us.

Our Father, Who art in Heaven, Who hast placed Thy store of mercy in Jesus Christ, our Priest, our Victim, our Altar, *forgive us our trespasses, as we forgive them that trespass against us.* Look upon the Face of Thy Christ imploring mercy for us, drawing down upon our souls Thy grace, Thy love, Thy favor, and forgive us.

What great need of purity and innocence I feel on approaching this Sacrament! What need I have of peace between Thee and me, between Thy Sanctity and my corruption! Father, have mercy on us, have mercy on me! *Kyrie eleison.*

In order to go to Thy Christ, in order to be as though fused in Him, in order to become "concorporate" and "consanguineous"[1] with Him, it is of urgent necessity that the same charity which fills Him and makes Him the Best-Beloved of Thy good-pleasure, should also fill me, making me an object worthy of Thy regard. Father, forgive us, forgive me all my sins, past and present!

As we forgive them that trespass against us. Lord Jesus, I enter into the very depths of my soul, trying to examine that secret chamber wherein Thou alone hast a right to enter, O my God, Thou Who art the *searcher of*

---

1 St Cyril of Jerusalem.

hearts and reins.[2] Humbly and to Thy glory, I confess that I see not nor am aware there of any bitterness toward anyone whatsoever. It seems to me I love all those Thou lovest, Lord, and desire for all of them that happiness of which I dream today for myself.

O my God, I forgive all who have ever injured me, all who, perhaps, lacking understanding of me, think, speak, or act against me. Thou seest them all, Lord; Thou forgivest them, doubtlessly; that I may forgive in my turn. Heap upon them, O Jesus, Thy tireless charity, Thy grace, even Thy choicest graces: I wish for them all the good I desire for myself, that Good above all good, Thyself, Lord, yes, Thy very Self!

It is the peculiar property, the special fruit of this Sacrament, to increase charity in the soul that receives it. What joy in the thought that the Bread of God, the Bread sublime, is going to strengthen the unity of the Body of the Church! This very day, in this approaching moment, the love of Christians for each other is going to be increased! And this love, renewed, augmented, more steadfast than ever, will be the victory of Christ Jesus in our souls and the establishment of His kingdom therein to the glory of our Heavenly Father!

---

2 Ps. 7: 10.

LXI
ET NE NOS INDUCAS IN TENTATIONEM
AND LEAD US NOT INTO TEMPTATION

Our Father Who art in Heaven, Thou invitest us, Thy children, to come to the sacred banquet of the Flesh and Blood of Christ, the banquet at which Thou wilt fill us with zeal for Thy glory, the banquet by virtue of which Thou aimest to bestow upon the powers of our souls the graces which turn us ever more truly toward Thee, our supreme goal. Ah, let us then come to Thee straightway, never again placing any obstacle in the way of Thy divine action! *Et ne nos inducas in tentationem!*

Temptation has its seat in my concupiscence, *the concupiscence of the flesh, and the concupiscence of the eyes, and the pride of life,* all those things which are *not of Thee,* O Father, *but of the world.*[1]

Create a clean heart in me, Father, *and renew a right spirit within my bowels,* that I may come to Jesus Christ: *Cor mundum crea in me, Deus.*[2] Quiet my corrupt flesh, a burden which innocence alone can lighten; subdue by Thy power the rebellion of this flesh, bring to naught its destructive influences; assimilate it, O Father, to that Flesh which it now prepares to receive, the Body of Thine immaculate Son; so may the union between the two be perfect, tranquil, and sweet and a breath of fragrance from the perfume of my chastity pervade the kiss of Jesus Christ in the moment of our meeting.

Our Father Who art in Heaven, free my heart from enchainment to things of this life, to the perishable, transitory, corruptible treasures of earth; let me not desire them; if I possess them, *let me use them as if I used them not, for the fashion of this world* passeth away,[3] *and it is in Heaven that I am to live,*[4] yes, in spirit even now, as if already I had joined Thee. After all, nothing would put a greater obstacle in the way of my fervor at the moment of Communion than an inordinate care for money, for wealth: Jesus wishes

---

1 1 John 2: 16.   2 Create a clean heart in me, O God (Ps. 50: 12).
3 1 Cor. 7: 31.   4 Phil. 3: 20.

to reign alone in my heart, its King and its treasure.

Lord Jesus, Thou hast said: *Learn of Me, because I am meek and humble.... Come to Me and I will refresh you.*[5] Oh, create in this heart which seeks Thee so sincerely that meekness and humility. Then wilt Thou grant my desire; then wilt Thou hasten to come to me; then wilt Thou open to me the springs of Life Which Thou art; then wilt Thou give me the Bread come down from Heaven, and still my thirst at Thy holy wounds with the Precious Blood which was my salvation.

Let neither the flesh, nor wealth, nor pride—that triple temptation of our fallen nature—continue to dominate my life: Come, O Flesh of Jesus Christ, spring forth, O Blood of my Saviour, that I may become more and more truly a new creature in Thee, *in Christo nova creatura.*[6]

So may nothing more arise during this most profound peace at the moment of our union, to disturb the free action of this love, a foretaste of Heaven!

---

5 Matt. 11: 28 and 29.   6 Cor. 5: 17.

LXII

SED LIBERA NOS A MALO

BUT DELIVER US FROM EVIL

Our Father, Who art in Heaven, lead us not into temptation: never again let us be the slaves of the flesh, of riches, of pride. These can not be of Thee, but come from the author of all evil, the "evil one," as he is called in the Scriptures, *in whom the whole world*—the world of the wicked—*is seated!*[1]

Deliver me, Lord, from the *evil one,* the source of all evil, physical and moral, from evil in every form, forasmuch as it appears, at any rate, Thine enemy and mine. Deliver us, deliver me from all evil!

In order to go to Jesus Christ, Thy supreme Good and my own Good, in order to partake of His infinite goodness, the source of all goodness on earth, I have such need of peace, security, good influences! Deliver me from evil, O Father Who lovest me!

I need so greatly to feel myself surrounded by the holy influence of Thine Angels, those whom Thou hast given charge over my life, *to keep me in all my ways.*[2]

Holy Angel of God, my guardian, to whose care the infinite goodness of God has entrusted me, enlighten me, watch over me, guide me, govern me! Let me follow thee to the holy Table, whither Thou precedest me in order to adore Him Whom I am going to receive. Instruct me and let me keep thy words in my heart!

Deliver me from evil, Father, *from all evils, past, present, and to come,*[3] from painful memories, present apprehensions and anxieties, and from fears for the future. I beseech Thee, *by the intercession of Mary,* the holy Mother of Jesus, who crushed beneath her immaculate foot the head of the infernal serpent, *by Thy blessed Apostles Peter and Paul,* who destroyed his reign

---

1   1 John 5: 19.   2   Ps. 90: 11.   3   The prayer *Libera nos* of the Mass.

on the earth, *by St Andrew*, whom Jesus loved "in the odor of sweetness," *in odorem suavitatis*,[4] and by *all Thy Saints*, sworn enemies of the spirit of darkness and confusion, to grant us peace, Thy peace, peace with my brothers, peace in my soul, in my body; let me, at peace in all my being, hasten eager, joyous, ardent, to my tryst with Him *Who is our real Peace, Ipse enim est Pax nostra.*[5]

Let the splendor of Thy mercy shine full upon us; it is *our help* in this solemn moment, and to it we abandon ourselves in complete confidence, hope, and love, *ut ope misericordice tuce adjuti.*[6]

Deliver us from evil, from the evil of sin; in final analysis, that is the only evil there is, since it is the only one that offends Thee. Deliver us from sin, from every vice, every imperfection. Let us be able to approach Jesus, the Purity of Virgins, with hearts chaste, detached from creatures, and humble, humble with the simple humility of little children, *for whom is the kingdom of Heaven;*[7] that is the kingdom which Thine Apostle defines as: *peace and joy in the Holy Ghost.*[8]

Lord Jesus, Thou didst Thyself teach us this prayer, didst help us to falter forth the Name of *our Father Who is in Heaven*. Always, with Thee, I shall repeat it at the altar of God; but, that I may say it effectively, put in my heart the dispositions that fill Thine own, O sublime Son of *our Father Who is in Heaven!*

---

4 Office of St Andrew. 5 For He is our Peace (Eph. 2: 14).
6 That aided by the help of Thy mercy...
7 Matt. 19: 14. 8 Rom. 14: 17.

LXIII

PAX DOMINI SIT SEMPER VOBISCUM

THE PEACE OF THE LORD BE ALWAYS WITH YOU

This formula, the expression of an ardent desire, was in olden times the signal for the *kiss of peace* which both ministers and faithful, the whole Christian assembly, were wont to celebrate in acknowledgment of that unity which remains, in Christianity, the last word in sanctity. This wish addressed to all of us by the priest has lost nothing today of its signification. It seems to admonish us: Love one another; be but one heart and one soul; be merged into one body! Lo, Jesus Christ comes, the Love which is to set you aflame.

It is while his holy and venerable hands hold the Body of Christ over the Precious Blood that the priest cries out to us: *The peace of the Lord be always with you!* And who among you, if charity were perhaps unknown in his heart, if he were not, heart and soul, one with his priest and with his brothers participating in the awe-inspiring Sacrifice, would dare, with this Precious Blood before his eyes, to make response: *And this peace be with thy spirit!* This is a frightful thought; one might call it a profanation of *this Blood, through which peace is made on earth and in Heaven.*[1]

After invoking Peace with this most holy Particle and inviting souls to the kiss of peace by it, I, priest of Jesus, put it then *into the chalice of everlasting salvation.* A wonderful symbol this! The sacramental species, *the holy things,* were separate until this moment to show the death of Jesus; now, the reunion of this Body and this Blood recall the glorious life He won in His Resurrection.

It is this glorious Christ I am about to receive, this Christ, just as I adore Him, reigning triumphant amid the splendors of the saints. It is this glorious Christ, the Life eternal, Whose Body and Blood consumed by me will

---

1 Col. 1: 20.

implant in my entire being—that is the hope expressed in the Postcommunion prayers—the seeds of the promised harvest of eternal Life.

If I receive often—every day if possible—the Flesh of the Son of God, if I drink His Blood, I also shall go forward to my future resurrection; I shall prepare it, shall receive the increase of its power. Ah, but I begin even now to participate in this eternal Life! Some transformation seems to be taking place within me, little by little; I am abandoning the way of Life of the old Adam and am adopting the morality of Jesus Christ, Prince of glory! How great a mystery is the Holy Eucharist! And what consolation there is in this Mystery of faith, what power is concealed within it!

It seems to have reached its culmination in this *Commixtion* or mingling, which is, in a way, another *Consecration* of the Body and the Blood of Jesus. Not that there is anything lacking in the first Consecration already entirely accomplished! Let us not forget that! But here, by reason of this mingling of the two species, by reason of their mutual attachment, their immediate contact, their reunion, there takes place an inter-consecration of their whole value, their complete virtue, their full power over our souls, an august inter-consecration of both, so to speak.

Who can comprehend things so exalted! And nevertheless they are here to draw down in this moment all the sanctity of Jesus to us who are going to receive this Body and this Blood, the Bread of eternal Life, *haec Commixtio et consecratio fiat accipientibus nobis in vitam aeternam.*[2] Amen.

---

2 May this mingling and consecration be unto us that receive it effectual unto life everlasting.

LXIV

AGNUS DEI, DONA NOBIS PACEM

LAMB OF GOD ... GRANT US PEACE

Jesus, Lamb of God, Who takest away the sins of the world, hidden Deity, I adore Thee devoutly.[1] Now the hour has arrived, the blessed hour, when Thou wilt vouchsafe to fill to the utmost the deep hunger of my soul and give it to drink of the rushing torrent of Thy pleasure, *et torrente voluptatis tuae potabis eos.*[2]

Lamb of God, of our Father Who is in Heaven, *have mercy on us*, have mercy on me! Thou, the Well-Beloved Son of this Father Who loves us, Thou comest to us, Thou wilt come to me, to pour into my heart some measure of that love which fills Thy Heart to overflowing for Him Who eternally begets Thee. Take from us, take from me, all fear of God; let me who come to Thee now, Lord Jesus, who hide myself in Thee, let me become also, but with Thee, the Well-beloved of the Father Who is in Heaven! It is for this reason I cry out: *Lamb of God, have mercy on us!*

Lamb of God, it is Thou Who hearest the sins of the world: Thou didst wish to take upon Thyself the load of sin which, from the time of Adam, our first father, has accumulated and risen to a fearful mountain before the Face of God. A moment ago, when Thine immolation was reenacted, Thou didst wash these sins away again, Lord, in order that we, sure of Thy pardon and of our purification, might seat ourselves in our wedding garments at the Father's table and receive His Bread, receive Thee, Lamb of God! I am aware, O infinite Purity, that my soul always has need of this pardon, this purification; *Lamb of God, have mercy!*

Lamb of God Who takest away the sins of the world, have mercy on us! Ah, let this cry of hope ring out for us amid the splendors of the saints, in the Heaven of Thy glory! May Thy saints, who were wont to make this sup-

---

1 *Adoro te.*
2 And Thou shalt make them drink of the torrent of Thy pleasure (Ps. 35: 9).

plication on earth, now make it for us in the clear light of Thy Beatitude, Lamb of God, Thou Who fillest them with Thyself as food and drink, Thou Whom we contemplate only in the light of faith!

Lamb of God Who takest away the sins of the world, have mercy on us! We send up this cry in union with the Church suffering, for whose relief we shall receive Thee, in order that she, for her part, may receive at this banquet the gifts of light and refreshment which she awaits therefrom.

Lamb of God Who takest away the sins of the world, grant us peace! The Church Militant cries out to Thee by all her children, and for all her children, united in this Sacrifice! Grant us, grant me peace, Thy supreme gift; peace, Thy kiss, pledge of Thy mercy and forgiveness; peace with God, our Father in Heaven, with our brethren, with all who may enjoy with me the Life eternal that Thou art. *Grant us peace;* may we come to Thee as members of a single body, one in Thee, our supreme Head, our souls abounding in love, eager to receive the Bread of Life which conquers death. *Lamb of God!*

LXV

PACEM MEAM DO VOBIS

MY PEACE I GIVE UNTO YOU

Lord Jesus Christ, Thou couldst give me no more special grace at this moment in which Thou vouchsafest to make Thyself the sustenance of my soul: peace. *My peace I give unto thee,* Thou sayest to me; Thou givest it me like a kiss of Thy mouth,[1] like a sign of Thy pleasure in me, and that in spite of the wretchedness Thou most surely seest in the fathomless depths of my nothingness.

My peace I give unto thee, my Heart's gift, which I desire to be thy supreme good in the hour when I bend over thee to take possession of all thy forces and fill them with the sweetness of my presence.

My peace I give unto thee, O soul of My priest, I would give it thee plenteous, measureless, perfect; the Sacrifice thou hast offered today in abundance of faith and love and with the tears of true contrition has found acceptance in My Father's sight. Thou canst ask no stronger proof thereof than this gift of peace which I make to thee, My peace, the peace of Jesus thy Christ, Who is Priest, Victim, and Altar with thee in this Sacrifice which bestows peace, the Sacrifice of My Body and My Blood.

My peace I give unto thee, the peace which the world desires not, which it disdains. But receive it thou, at least; welcome it as the companion that will guide thee to the holy wound of thy God, to that place of rest where the saints enjoy the unspeakable union that is the reward of their confidence.

Peace of God, Lord Jesus, I come to Thee with the self-abandonment demanded by Thy love; I put my trust under the covert of Thy wings. No, *look not upon my sins;* Thou hast but now washed them away in Thy Precious Blood; look only *upon the faith of Thy Church,* the faith of each of

---

[1] Cant. 1: 1.

her members, the faith of Thy priest who, in the name of all, confesses that Thou art *the Lamb of God Who grantest forgiveness and peace.*

O Christ, Peace of Heaven and of earth, so fill me with Thyself that the stream of Thy sweetness shall overflow and surge onward to all the souls who come today to Thy holy Table to receive Thy gift, to be nourished by it, and find in its celestial delights the sweet remedy for all the bitterness of earth.

Yes, *vouchsafe peace to Thy Church,* Thou, true Peace of the children of God; establish her members in charity, weld them into unity, such unity as Thou, Jesus, desiredst for them, when, on the last evening of Thy mortal life, Thou madest supplication to Thy Heavenly Father, saying: *Holy Father, keep these whom Thou hast given me, that they may be one, that they may be made perfect, that they all may be one as Thou, Father, in Me, and I in Thee, that they also may be one in Us, in order that the world may believe that Thou hast sent Me.*[2]

O Jesus, I receive Thy Kiss in fullness of joy! May Thy most merciful grace make it possible to me and to all who receive Thy Kiss at this Sacrifice today—make it possible to our love—to make amends for the sacrilegious kiss of Judas; in this way mayest Thou be consoled and blessed by the faithfulness of Thy friends, the faithful at the daily rendezvous, by those whom Thou desirest to be the *peaceful children* of Thy Father, heirs of that Peace Which Thou art, Lord, that Peace Which I receive when Thou sayest to me: My peace I give unto thee: not that which the world giveth, but Mine own.[3]

---

2 John 17: 11 *ff.*   3 John 14: 27.

LXVI

ME A TE NUNQUAM SEPARARI PERMITTAS

NEVER SUFFER ME TO BE SEPARATED FROM THEE

To be separated from Thee, Lord Jesus, is the most terrible disaster that can overtake any soul. Indeed, there is no other. What are all earthly sufferings compared with this, with the pain of being far from Thee, of belonging no more to Thee, of no longer rejoicing in Thee?

To be separated from Thee, Lord Jesus! The mere thought of that loss causes a tremor. Can there in truth be souls—even souls of priests, too!—that live thus detached from the divine trunk, from the Vine Which Thou art, souls that can consent to be branches cut off from Thy Life, O Jesus?

To be separated from Thee, Lord Jesus! Why, that were futility, emptiness, barrenness of life! Ah, more! It were death with its horror, death of the soul, beyond comparison more horrible than bodily death! And there are souls, souls of priests, that live thus?

To be separated from Thee, Lord Jesus! Then would there be indeed no apostolate more, no success more, no harvest of souls more. For without Thee I can do nothing, Thou hast said again and again.[1] No, my brothers, without the Lord Jesus we are powerless, abandoned to our native weakness, which lays our souls open to sin and its concupiscences; without the Lord Jesus we are nothing; we may appear to achieve results, to gain success, aye, even to do good, great good; but what is it all lacking Him without Whom we can do nothing!

And though we were simply members of the faithful, what are we, I ask you, what can we do, separated from the Lord Jesus? What of the branch which, torn from the live trunk, is lying on the ground, already rotting and covered with vermin, delivered to its own death? It is withering. What can

---

1 John 15: 4 *ff.*

we hope for separated from Jesus? What will become of us? We shall likewise wither and, gathered up like worthless vine-branches, shall be cast into the fire;[2] the fire which is unquenchable,[3] eternal, with the worm that dieth not:[4] a conscience, devoured with remorse, tortured by the consciousness of loss, a soul that must have known, must have experienced, and now knows, yes, eternally, what it means to be with the Lord Jesus!

Lord Jesus Christ, Who comest to me today, Who dost vouchsafe to give me in Thy Flesh and Thy Blood a pledge of eternal Life, *Lord Jesus, never suffer me to be separated from Thee, Who with God the Father and Holy Ghost livest and reignest God forever and ever!*

Thou didst die to give life to the world, to give life to me by Thy supreme Oblation. Thou hast left me the sublime Memorial of Thy blessed Passion, in order that, by means of Thy wondrous Sacrament, I may enter into possession of Thy Life, a Life which is to be eternal; in order that from now on I may abide in that Life in this valley of trial and tears. Never suffer me to be separated from Thee, neither in time nor in eternity.

Forgive me, if there is still need, all my iniquities, all my misdeeds, known or unknown; deliver me from the evil of living so far from Thee, even though it be but the separation of a moment! And, to that end, fill me with Thy fear, *pierce Thou my flesh therewith;*[5] make me cleave with unfailing faith to Thy holy law, the law of Thy Gospel. Let not the receiving of Thy Most Holy Sacrament, source of Life everlasting, turn to my judgment and damnation; no, rather *may it avail me for a safeguard and remedy both of soul and body* at times when my weaknesses would separate me from Thee.

Lord Jesus, let us never again be separated from each other; not for a single moment, neither by day nor by night; dost Thou not come to me to enjoy the delights of an abiding union?

---

2 John 15: 6.   3 Luke 3: 17.   4 Mark 9: 43.   5 Ps. 98: 120.

LXVII

DOMINE, NON SUM DIGNUS

LORD, I AM NOT WORTHY

Lord, I kneel before Thee, before Thee Who art *the Bread of Heaven, Which I will take, calling upon Thy Name.* Thy Name, O Jesus Christ, the Name which my faith adores, which my hope greets, which my love embraces, that Name is Mercy, Benignity, infinite Condescension toward the sinner, to whom Thou givest the sweet name of friend.[1] *Panem caelestem accipiam et Nomen Domini invocabo.*[2] O Jesus Christ, I kneel before Thee and I adore Thee!

Ecce Agnus Dei, ecce qui tollit peccata mundi.[3] Kneeling, I confess that beneath these lowly forms, bread and wine, Thou art my Saviour, the Lamb That was slain, Who once more descendest to give my soul abundantly of the *fruit of Thy Redemption* and enrich me with the graces which prepare for the Life eternal. *O Thou Who takest away the sins of the world, have mercy on me!*

Confiteor. Humbly I confess my sins to Almighty God, to the Blessed Virgin Mary, to all Thy saints; yes, I have sinned much, *exceedingly,* the Church makes me say, *quia peccavi nimis;* and it is through my fault, yes, through my fault, through my most grievous fault. O Virgin most pure, O St Michael, Angel of God, O Holy Apostles and Saints of the Lord, and you, my Father, minister, for me, of the divine largess, pray for me, the poor sinner, unworthy in every way of this visit of my God!

Domine, non sum dignus. No, Lord, I am not worthy that Thou shouldst enter under my roof. The centurion of the Gospel had reasons perhaps for these words; and yet by his faith, which even moved Thine own admiration, O Jesus, he seemed already to have advanced so far! I, on the contrary, after

---

1 John 15: 15.
2 I will take the Bread of Heaven and call upon The Name of the Lord.
3 Behold the Lamb of God, behold Him Who taketh away the sins of the world.

all the graces I have received—and used so badly!—must say in all truth: *Lord, I am not worthy!*

No, *Lord, I am not worthy*. Long years, heaped with innumerable instances of the provident care of Thine infinite mercy, have passed since the ever-blessed day of my First Holy Communion. So many times, thousands of times, Thou hast graciously come down into my heart. Since then, it would seem, I ought already to have been transformed into Thee, O Bread of Heaven! Alas! Every day I am more conscious of my profound misery, so that it is in all sincerity that I cry out to Thee: *Domine, non sum dignus.* Lord, I am not worthy.

After so many years in the priesthood, after having ascended to Thine altar thousands of times, after having renewed day after day the adorable Sacrifice which is all religion, after having held in my trembling hands, consecrated by Thee, this Holy Body, this most Precious Blood, Which Thy Seraphim adore, after all this, it would seem that I ought already to have imitated what I touched, *Imitamini quod tractatis;*[4] yes, surely, I should appear by this time Thy very image, O Jesus, an image of Thyself crucified that has been wholly transmuted into Thy spiritual beauty, like Thy saints! Alas, again, I have but just begun the reform of my entire being; therefore I implore Thee, repeating, *Lord, I am not worthy.*

Domine, non sum dignus. After all, who could be? Who could possibly be worthy to approach Thee and to receive in his soul Him Who can perceive imperfections in His very angels?

Seraphim and Cherubim of the Lord, who flame with love in His presence, you whom the Sun of Divinity illuminates with His flashing light, Angels of God, my holy Angel guardian, you are confounded and lost in the knowledge of your nothingness before this Splendor of the Father Who floods you with His glory and you confess your unworthiness to utter His Most Holy Name! Then I, poor sinner, what should I do but repeat again and yet again: *Lord, I am not worthy that Thou shouldst enter under my roof.*

Oh, say but the word, and my soul shall be healed! One word uttered by Thee was sufficient to create worlds and hurl them into space. One single *fiat*[5] of Thine caused light to spring forth from the darkness which held it captive! But what am I saying? Thou art this very Word, Word of the

---

4 *Pontificale Romanum:* Ordination of Priests.
5 *Fiat lux*, let there be light (Gen. 1: 3).

Father! Come forth from Thyself, O Word of my God; rest over my soul, shine upon its thick gloom; enlighten, strengthen my faith; awaken my hope, increase my love; and, once more, *Thou shalt renew the face of the earth.*[6]

Say the word. Say this most living word, which is *more piercing* than any *two-edged sword*, the word that penetrates the soul that listens for Thy divine accents; say *this word reaching even unto the division of the soul and the spirit, of the joints also and the marrow.*[7] Say it, Lord, and it shall suffice: my soul, visited by Thee, filled with Thy splendor and Thy love, shall be healed. It will be healed, once and for all, of its gloom, its weaknesses, its cowardices, for it will have seen the Salvation of God.[8] *Et sanabitur anima mea.*[9]

---

6 Ps. 103: 30.   7 Heb. 4: 12.   8 Luke 3: 6.
9 And my soul shall be healed.

LXVIII
CORPUS ... SANGUIS ... CHRISTI CUSTODIAT ANIMAM

MAY THE BODY AND BLOOD OF CHRIST KEEP MY SOUL

The mystery is accomplished. God descends into my nothingness and I am swallowed up in Him.

What shall I do? First of all I will be silent, Lord, and adore Thee within my soul.

Yes, let all tumult cease around me and within me! God in me, and I in God. The union is perfect: we are one now, Jesus and I, and through Him, with Him, in Him, I am united with the Father Who is in Heaven.

Let every creature be blotted from my sight: I see now only my Best-Beloved; in this deep silence which only the voice of God may break, my whole being implores of Him: *Osculetur me osculo oris sui*, that He kiss me with the kiss of His mouth.[1] O Lord Jesus, give me Thy kiss, Thy Holy Spirit and the Fire thereof, Thy love with which Thou art come to inebriate me; I ask nothing more.

Love, O my soul, love Thy Lord Jesus Christ in the love of the Father and of the Son! Abandon thyself to the influence of this charity divine; it is the special fruit of the holy gift of the Eucharist. Love Thy Love in love.

He that eateth My flesh and drinketh My blood abideth in Me, and I in him.[2] *The same beareth much fruit.*[3] *And this fruit he gathereth unto life everlasting, et congregat fructum in vitam aeternam.*[4] Today I eat and I drink eternal Life, the Life that is Jesus Christ, the true God, *Hic est verus Deus et Vita aeterna.*[5] I have just partaken this day of the food that yields immortality; immortality has been augmented and strengthened within me; then who shall separate me from Jesus Christ, my Life everlasting?

What return shall I make to the Lord for all He hath given unto me? I will

---

[1] Cant. 1: 1.   [2] John 6: 57.   [3] John 15: 5.   [4] John 4: 36.
[5] This is the true God and Life eternal (1 John 5: 20).

take the Chalice of salvation and call upon the Name of the Lord. Praising I will call upon the Lord and I shall be saved from my enemies—the enemies of immortality.[6]

O Body and Blood of Jesus Christ, I adore Thee in the fullness of my faith, for my senses are in complete darkness; I see nothing, taste nothing; my vision is wholly interior; by faith alone I seize upon Thee; Thy sweetness is within my soul; I wait for Thee to speak and reveal Thyself, Lord Jesus, Thyself to myself. *Credo quidquid dixit Dei Filius.*[7]

Meanwhile, let me desire Thee with the intensity of desire Thou createst within me; let me pray to Thee, Bread of eternal Life, Wine that gladdens my heart! Let me implore Thee in this sacred and most solemn moment of my day!

Anima Christi, sanctifica me! Soul of Christ, sanctify me! I adore Thee, O Thou Holy of Holies, Thou divine Plenitude and Abyss of graces!

Sanctify Thou me, O Sanctity of God; for art Thou not the soul of the Incarnate Word, of Him Who is uncreated Sanctity, by Whose grace Thou enterest into the union which makes Thee the soul of a God!

Sanctify Thou me, O uncreated Sanctity, overflowing with that fullness of graces which makes saints of us, too, that measureless Fullness *of which we have all received.*[8]

Sanctify Thou me, O Soul of Jesus Christ, with Thine own Sanctity, with that Sanctity into which all Thy saints pass when, giving Thee their souls, they receive Thine into themselves, that Thy mind may be in them, O Jesus Christ, *sentite in vobis, quod et in Christo Jesu.*[9]

Make me Thy holy one, O Holy Soul! Only this one grace I ask of Thee—if indeed there be any grace beside this one that is not really meant to make me Thy Saint. Make holy my soul and all the powers of my being: my memory, my intelligence, my will, my liberty; make holy my desires, my joys, my sufferings, and my trials.

Sanctify Thou me in my body; immerse it in Thine abysmal purity, O Jesus, Purity of Virgins, that it may truly be the instrument of my soul, and that both may strive together toward the likeness of Thy Sanctity. Soul of Christ, sanctify me!

---

6 Prayer of the Mass.
7 I believe whatever the Son of God hath said (*Adoro te*).   8 John 1: 16.
9 For let this mind be in you which was also in Christ Jesus (Phil. 2: 5).

Corpus Christi, salva me! Body of Christ, save me! I adore Thee, Body of my God, Bread of Angels which feeds all who are hungry for God!

I adore Thee, glorious Humanity of Jesus Christ, That, visiting my soul and my body, implantest in them the seed of immortality! Body of Christ, invade my being, permeate the very bone and marrow of my own body; quicken all my blood and accomplish therein the work of grace and glory!

Save me, Body of Jesus Christ, the same, Thou, that, made flesh in the Virgin Mary, didst really suffer, wast truly immolated for men, for me, on the holy Cross!

Save me, Body of Jesus Christ, sacred Body, pierced that the Blood and Water, gushing forth, might show the wound of Love in Thy Heart and throw open the way that leads to the depths of this great Heart of Love.

Save me, Body of Christ, Body most chaste, Body most pure, virginal Body That teachest, nourishest, and protectest Thy virgins! O Jesus, my most sweet Love, O Jesus, full of mercy, O Jesus, Son of Mary, save me!

Sanguis Christi, inebria me! Blood of Christ, inebriate me! I have put my lips to Thy celestial cup and have felt my soul and body invaded by the infinite sweetness of Thy divinity. I was athirst for Thee, my God, and Thou earnest to quicken my life; yet even so my thirst grows and will consume me. For art Thou not the Torrent of pleasure[10] which is infinite and therefore inexhaustible?

Blood of Christ, inebriate me! Lord Jesus, loving Pelican, Thou Who didst tear Thy breast, yes, Who yet ceaselessly tearest it, to feed our little souls, look upon this poor sinner, who, humbled though he is, nevertheless raises himself up to reach Thy blessed wound and receive of that Fountain of Life everlasting,[11] to drink in that divine liquid whereof one single drop can still save worlds.[12]

Blood of Christ, inebriate me! Free me from concupiscence of every kind; separate me from all creatures; quench the ardor of the impure blood that surges in my veins, and implant in them the fire of Thy Holy Spirit, that they may flow with Thy sacred Wine, the inebriating Wine of Thy Love!

Aqua lateris Christi, lave me! Water from the side of Christ, wash me! Lord, Thou gavest all: Thy Sacred Heart kept nothing for itself, not even this Water which constantly flows forth and which I am this moment ea-

---

10 Ps. 35: 9.   11 John 4: 14.   12 *Adoro te.*

gerly drinking, as it mingles with this Precious Blood, with which it is Thy loving will I be inebriated. Every morning Thou remindest me of the completeness of Thy Sacrifice when, at the offertory of the Holy Mass, I pour with tremulous hand the drop of water which is lost in the wine of sacrifice.

Water from the side of Jesus Christ, wash me, purify me, make me immaculate, restore to me, to Thy priest who, alas, can himself be contaminated with the dust of the earth, restore and preserve to him the robe of shining whiteness with which Thou desirest him always to be clothed at the hour of the holocaust. For shall he not reflect the whiteness of Thy Host, of Thy very Self, O Jesus, Who art the radiant Light of the heavenly Jerusalem?

Passio Christi, conforta me! O Passion of Christ, strengthen me! I have just celebrated Thy mystery, I have just announced Thy death anew, O Jesus, and therewith all Thy sufferings as the Victim of the Father. Now the moment is come for me to *imitate what I have touched*,[13] *Imitamini quod tractatis*. Henceforth I must go my way clothed in Jesus crucified; His Body and His Blood which I have offered, and of which I have received, must mark me with the most holy character of His blessed Passion. Only at this price shall I glorify my Lord; only at this price will souls acknowledge me their priest; only at this price shall I obtain the right to immolate them one by one at the altar in order to make of these victims of God, the crown of honor of the Passion of my Lord and Saviour.

O divine Passion of my Jesus, strengthen me! Strengthen me in my struggles, in my lassitudes, in my weaknesses! Let the memory of Thee never leave me, that I may ever be transformed to the likeness of Jesus crucified! With Him as my sustenance, I possess thee entirely, holy Passion of Jesus Christ, and thou art my single treasure!

O bone Jesu, exaudi me! Hear me, I pray, O good Jesus, Son of the Father, Lover of souls, only Hope of my soul!

Intra tua vulnera absconde me! In Thy holy wounds hide me! Thy wounds, Lord Jesus, wounds of Thy hands which so often blessed, wounds of Thy feet which trod such weary ways, and, oh, the wide wound in Thy side, wherefrom Thy saints of Heaven and earth drink so eagerly! These wounds, Lord Jesus, Thy priests do not contemplate enough; Thy friends do not

---

13 *Pontificale Romanum:* Ordination of Priests.

press into them so eagerly as they ought. Yet in them lies a treasure, the exhaustless treasure of God.

Quite fresh are these wounds of Thine to my eyes, Lord Jesus, and I offer them to Thee as if for the first time! Thy wounds are a road, oh, so simple and easy a road, by which to travel to Heaven! They are an ocean, the harbors of which are large enough to hold the earth, and purgatory, and Heaven! Within Thy wounds hide me, O good Jesus!

Ne Permittas me separari a Te! Suffer me never to be separated from Thee, Lord Jesus! That would be frightful! Then were Thy Blood shed in vain, then were Thy holy Passion without effect, then were Thy Work a failure, Lord Jesus crucified! No, let any suffering be mine; but to be separated from Thee, not only in eternity but even in this world of time; to be separated from Thee here on earth if only for an instant, ah, no, never, never! Rather would I die a thousand deaths than that death, the only death there is, the only death I have to fear.

Ab hoste maligno defende me! From the malicious enemy defend me, from the wiles of Satan, from his sacrilegious cunning! Defend me from his suggestions, which would aim at no less thing than the destruction of the work accomplished in my soul today by Thy Holy Eucharist! Defend me from his pride, his rebellions, his baseness! Spirit of Jesus, Spirit of sweetness and humility, Spirit of simplicity, which is the appanage of Thy little children, Spirit of Jesus received by me in Thy Body and Thy Blood, defend Thou me!

In hora mortis meae voca me! In the hour of my death call me, Lord Jesus, God of the Eucharist! Was not Thy Most Holy Sacrament instituted to serve as provision for soul and body on their pilgrimage to eternity? Call me, O good Jesus, when suffering shall hold me fast, when the death agony shall seize me, when my eyes shall be glazed, and I shall no longer be able to see the wound in Thy blessed side. Call me then; let me hear Thy sweet voice, the voice of my Friend, my Spouse, my beloved Master, the sole Hope of my heart.

Et jube me venire ad Te! And bid me come to Thee, Lord Jesus! If I tremble then; if I should doubt; if, remembering my sins, I should hesitate to rush with complete confidence and love to Thy wound to be drawn therein and cast into Thy mighty Heart of Love; ah, then, command me! force me then to come to Thee as I came on the day of my First Communion, and on the day of my first Sacrifice, as I have come so many times in my life, drawn by the charms of Thine unspeakable delights. Command me, and I shall come, breathing forth my soul in Thy kiss, O Jesus, and singing the praise of Thy wounds in the canticle of Thy saints: *Vulnera tua, merita mea,* Thy wounds, O Lord, are my merits! Have mercy on Thy priest!

Ut cum sanctis tuis laudem Te in saecula saeculorum. That with Thy saints I may praise Thee forever and ever! That I, having been Thy "Sacrifice of praise" at the altar, may now be forever Thy "Hymn of glory" in the presence of Thy Majesty.

Amen! Yes, may it so be! And thus *may the Body and the Blood of Our Lord Jesus Christ preserve my soul unto Life everlasting. Amen! Fiat, fiat!*

LXIX

UT IN ME NON REMANEAT MACULA

THAT NO STAIN OF SIN MAY REMAIN IN ME

Thy wondrous *Gift* is mine, Lord, and this free Gift, this measureless Treasure is Thyself. I possess Thee, the God-Man; I possess Thy Divinity, that Divinity Thy Seraphim adore from the glowing depths of their burning love; I possess Thy sacred Humanity, Thy Soul wholly beautiful in the light of the divine truths wherein it bathes, Thy Body agleam with the fires of glory; I possess Thy Being entire, Thee, the Incarnate Word, Redeemer of the world! Henceforth, for me, this Gift will be my help to immortality, an eternal remedy, *fiat nobis remedium sempiternum*.[1] What a remedy, and how necessary it is that I make use of it!

Therefore I pray Thee, Lord Jesus, Thee Who art this Gift of God, the living Eucharist, the eternal remedy of my own being, I implore Thee to cause *Thy Body which I have received and Thy Blood which I have drunk to cleave unto my inmost parts*[2] as a divine antidote to preserve me from sin, to forewarn me against its attacks, and save me from its snares.

The inmost parts of my soul are my memory, my intelligence, and my will, faculties capable of all good but also of all evil—capable of the one evil that includes all others, sin. *Redime me et miserere mei!* Lord, have mercy, again and always, mercy!

I consecrate my memory to Thee in this moment. Let it be Thy dwelling place, O Jesus, Thy holy dwelling, full of peace, full of recollections of Thy mercies to me. Drive therefrom all that might cloud it, besmirch it, trouble it; fill it, O Eucharist of God, with Thy divine clarity, with Thy purity, with Thine ineffable silence, in order that, giving itself ever more to the recollection of Thy presence within it, it may become the receptacle of more and more sublime gifts.

---

1 May it become to us an everlasting healing (The first ablutions).
2 The last ablutions.

I consecrate my intelligence to Thee, O Jesus. Is not Thy Holy Eucharist given to pour Thy Light into it, the Light which is Thyself, the Light which will guide it forward on the way of faith, to reveal to it at last the vision of the Lord of Powers? Then dissipate all its darkness, drive from it all obscurity; let it be always illuminated by Thy fires, O shining Beacon That enlightenest little ones, the humble, *et revelasti ea parvulis.*[3]

I consecrate my will to Thee. Enter Thou into the depths of my heart; fill it with Thy sweetness; let it ever thirst for Thee alone; and let it thus come to feel the constant and urgent desire to follow after Thee with the generous abandon that triumphs over every rebellious impulse, *ad te nostras etiam rebellas compelle propitius voluntates.*[4]

These inmost parts of my soul I consecrate to Thee; therefore they are Thine from this moment; that is to say, Thou hast dominion over them now, not sin, whose reign is over. *Non ergo regnet peccatum in vestro mortali corpore.*[5] Reign Thou, Lord Jesus, in these inmost parts of my soul, that they may never more *obey carnal desires.* Let no trace of this sin remain in them; but let grace keep them instead in Thy dominion. Thou hast but now strengthened these inmost powers. Behold them now at Thy feet, eager to serve Thee and *to be about Thy Father's business.*[6] Oh, let the virtue of Thy *pure and holy* gift, the Eucharist, so act upon them that the restoration of peace may be wrought in my soul, in this soul which has sought Thee, Thee Who art Peace, Who art the only Peace of men, *quem pura et sancta refecerunt sacramenta.*[7]

Remain with Thy priests, O Jesus, remain with all who have partaken today of Thy Body and Thy Blood, wherever they may be! The most holy Species will be consumed within me in a moment but the *virtue,* the secret power of this Eucharist, will not leave *me;* it will dwell in the sanctuary of my soul to work therein miracles of grace and prepare therein the wonders of eternal glory. In this wise Thou canst be always with me, O God of the Eucharist, and always with Thee! What a dream—or, rather, what reality!

---

3 Thou hast revealed Them to little ones (Luke 10: 21).
4 Even though our wills rebel, mercifully compel them to follow the behests of Thy will (*Secret* of the Fourth Sunday after Pentecost).
5 Let not sin therefore reign in your mortal body so as to obey the lusts thereof (Rom. 6: 12).
6 Luke 2: 49.   7 Whom Thy pure and holy mysteries have refreshed.

LXX

MORTEM DOMINI ANNUNTIABITIS

YOU SHALL SHOW FORTH THE DEATH OF THE LORD

These words, which have already been heard at the beginning of the Holy Sacrifice[1] and which epitomize the mystery of the Eucharist, are now repeated and sung while the priest distributes to the faithful who have gathered the Gift of God, the Body and the Blood which give eternal Life. The priest, more than they, draws sustenance from the meaning of these words as from a precious grace which leads the soul to a strong resolution.

Filled with the sweetness of the adorable Sacrament we, passing thereby into the sublime functions of Jesus as Priest, Victim, and Altar of His Sacrifice, have now all of us to live accordingly. *Imitamini quad tractatis:*[2] we must imitate what we touch. We must imitate Jesus, especially in His death which we have just announced, and, especially, therefore, in His character of *Host*, or Victim. We announce the Passion, the death of the Lord; then we must appear veritably in the eyes of God and our brethren like dead, whose life is hid with Christ in God![3] There is no truer statement than that.

Fix thy gaze, O my soul, upon this Host now reigning and radiant in thyself, in the depths of Thy being, and strive to be like Him.

This Host, this Victim, is the Word of God, the Word Which speaks forever, Which speaks by His very essence, being the Word of the Father; and nevertheless, here He is silent, utterly effaced beneath the most holy Species. Learn thou, also, to be silent; from the silence of Thy God learn to live.

This Host, God Himself, Thou sawest at the altar, inert, motionless, as if fastened to the altar on which He lay, wholly subject to the will of the priest who was offering Him as Victim. He even allowed Himself to be consumed, to be made a complete sacrifice! He has even suffered profanation! Be thou like Him: give thyself up, abandon thyself to His Father Who is also thine;

---

1 In the Epistle.
2 *Pontificale Romanum:* Ordination of Priests.   3 Col. 3: 3.

ask nothing, refuse nothing, give full sway to the Love That has chosen thee to be a victim in union with the divine Victim. Be as it were dead to all things, and never wilt thou live so intensely.

The Host is white. Ah, my Jesus, art Thou not the spotless Lamb That movest Heaven and earth to rapt adoration? So dazzling is Thy perfect whiteness, so blindingly reflected from the wings of Thy glowing Cherubim and Thy Seraphim flaming with love! Be thou pure, O my soul! Renounce wholeheartedly every creature; do not sully the receptacle which is resplendent this moment with the incomparable beauty of the Sacred Host it contains.

In His substance the divine Victim remains hidden beneath the accidents which conceal Him: I have just received this substance, and was conscious only of the taste of bread, the taste of wine; yet I partook of the Body and of the Blood of the Son of God! O mystery of mysteries! And I myself shall become at last nothing more than the accidents of Jesus; I shall become more and more like these forms beneath which He deigns to conceal Himself. But, in very truth in my inmost being will be *not I, but Jesus living in me.*[4]

O death which art Life! O Passion of my Saviour, which becomest the Resurrection of Jesus Christ in me! Again and again, better and better, I would announce thee. If I did not do so, I should be but an unworthy guest at the holy table to which Jesus so graciously invited me today. Yes, unworthy.

O my God, let it never happen that I should go even farther: that I should ever profane Thy Body and Thy Blood, that I should eat Thy Flesh and drink Thy Blood in sin and thus eat and drink my own condemnation, *reus erit Corporis et Sanguinis Domini.*[5] That would be crucifying Thee again. Lord, forgive in Thy mercy all who crucify Thee thus!

---

4 Gal. 2: 20.
5 He shall be guilty of the Body and of the Blood of the Lord (1 Cor. 11: 27).

LXXI

DIVINITATIS TUAE SEMPITERNA FRUITIONE[1]

GRANT US, O LORD, THAT ETERNAL ENJOYMENT OF THY GODHEAD

The effect of all the Sacraments is to produce special fruits in the souls of all who receive them. The special fruit of the Holy Eucharist is charity; for this very reason it is called the Sacrament of Love. To be sure, it presupposed love; but it was given to us in order to increase this love to such a degree as to perfect within us that holiness which is simply the union of the soul with God.

Then Thy Holy Eucharist, Lord Jesus, which is simply Thyself, the divine Victim, is a symbol, a living symbol, of heavenly beatitude. What shall we do in Heaven? We shall be immersed in the Ocean of beatitude which is God, God the Triune, Who is at once Father, Son, and Spirit of Love; we shall be engulfed in the splendor of the Word, Who is the Wisdom of the Father and the indefectible Light of this Blessed Trinity; we shall contemplate with ecstatic joy His sacred Humanity, through which, as through a sublime prism, this Word diffuses the plenitude of His Light; we shall rejoice in Mary, the Immaculate, in all the saints of Jesus, in whom He lives on forever. In a word we shall be filled—*fac nos repleri*.[2] But of this plenitude which will be ours in the empyreal glory we are already given the beginnings here below in the torrents of grace which stream into our souls from the Holy Eucharist, that is, from the Lord Jesus.

Yes, even here on earth I know God, love God, knowing and loving Jesus the Sacred Host. My intelligence, illuminated by the living light of faith is singularly quickened by His mystery. I do not yet see Him with my bodily vision, but the eyes of my soul discern Him. They discern, in so far as an

---

1 *Postcommunion* of Corpus Christi. 2 Grant that we be filled.

earthly creature can comprehend it, the Truth which is Jesus. The Holy Eucharist it is that enlightens all the saints of Jesus, leading them little by little, according to the measure of their faith, into the endless vastness of His knowledge. It is the Eucharist which gives them the power to measure *the breadth, and length, and height, and depth of this knowledge which fills unto all the fullness of God.*[3]

But if the Holy Eucharist can make Cherubim, those princes of knowledge, even here on earth, It creates the Seraphim also, those fires of love which burn before the Face of God and are consumed in His charity. The Holy Eucharist is the delight of souls who not only understand the Truth, but who are afire with love; it is the delight of souls who touch God, who experience God, who taste, savor, and drink of the torrent of pleasure, which in Heaven will come to full flood.

Ah, my soul, why dost thou still seek thy Heaven on high, since thou findest it in the tabernacle and on the altar? What am I saying? Heaven is in thy heart, since Jesus the Host reigns there, bestowing upon it ever more bountiful gifts of His sweetness, the sweetness that surpasses all understanding.

The saints of Heaven contemplate the divine Essence, they adore the Word, they are rapt in the Vision of their God; and all this is theirs by the Light of Glory.[4] But on earth, O my soul, thou canst contemplate even now by the light of faith the Light divine, at least in such degree as this gift falls to thy lot. In both cases it is the same Jesus, the same Word, the same God, given world with out end.

Lord Jesus, let me hide my unworthiness beneath the fiery wings of Thy Seraphim; and now whilst I await the revelation of Thy glorious Countenance, whilst I look forward to seeing Thee with my own eyes, to drinking in peace my fill of Thy sweetness, let me be ravished away by Thy beauty from all the passing show of earth, until at last I may enjoy Thee forever and forever!

---

3 Eph. 3: 18 and 19.
4 The *lumen gloriae:* St Thomas, *Summa Theologica, I, Quaest.* XII, Art. V. (Translator).

LXXII
PLACEAT TIBI SANCTA TRINITAS

MAY THE HOMAGE OF MY SERVICE
BE PLEASING TO THEE, O HOLY TRINITY

I adore Thee, O Holy Trinity of the Father, of the Son, and of the Holy Ghost, and my being is engulfed in Thy presence. I am nothingness effacing itself before the All, the formless atom confessing its Creator. Most Holy Trinity, I thank Thee, that Thou hast brought me to the fulfillment of my august ministry. I have offered unto Thee Jesus Christ, the sublime Victim Who enraptures Heaven and earth. Thou hast accepted this supreme oblation, the only one pleasing to Thee, the only one with which my soul could be united to be offered also unto Thee. Now it is time to conclude the mystery of the *Great Action,* and I bow low before Thy glory, a last time imploring Thy mercy. *Placeat tibi!*[1]

Grant that the Sacrifice which I, though unworthy, have offered be acceptable to Thee! Ah, why should it not be so, O Blessed Trinity, since Thou sawest, O Father, in Thy servant none other than Thy Best-Beloved! For I myself was hidden in God Who is my Christ and had become, through Him, with Him, in Him, priest and victim in my turn. Jacob put on the more beautiful garb of Esau, the First-born, and Thou hast *smelled the fragrant smell of the garments of Thy Son,* my Lord Jesus Christ.[2]

Ah, more than ever, Holy Father, see now in my poor self only Him, Thy High Priest, our Saviour! Word of the Father, see only Thy holy Humanity prostrate before Thee, supporting in itself my weaknesses. O Spirit of the Father and the Son, see only this sublime Priest and all the love—a God-Man's love—which He poured forth in the most holy Action, which alone gives due honor to the Trinity of the Father, of the Son, and of the Holy Ghost. *Placeat tibi obsequium servitutis meae!*[3]

---

1 May it be pleasing unto Thee.   2 Gen. 27: 27.
3 May the performance of my homage be pleasing to Thee.

Permit moreover, in Thy mercy, that this sacrifice be profitable to our imperfect piety, so little corresponding with such sublimity! May it benefit Thy priest and all for whom I have offered it; may it win forgiveness for us all! And as I begin this morning the new day Thou hast granted me that in it I may advance in sanctity—in the sanctity that beseems Thy priests, let this holocaust offered exclusively unto Thy glory gain Thy favor for my prayer and crown my just desires! So great need have I of Thee, O my God, almighty Father, divine Wisdom, compassionate Love!

May my sacrifice be of benefit to Thy Church so dear, to all the members of Jesus Christ, and particularly to those whom, by Thine unspeakable condescension, Thou hast confided to my care, as a pledge of love.

May it be of benefit both to the living and to all the faithful departed; may every imploring soul receive of the Precious Blood of the Lamb poured from this Chalice and gather the fruit of Thine unutterable goodness, O Thrice-Holy God!

With tenderness I kiss the altar stone whereon this Blood has just been shed once more to the praise and glory of Thy Name, for the benefit of Thy Church and all of Thine elect. I receive therefrom Thy last blessing streaming with graces, *O Trinity of Blessed Light, O Unity of princely might.*[4] I lift my hands up toward Heaven in supplication and clasping them again, I bless all who are Thine *in the Name of the Father, and of the Son, and of the Holy Ghost.*

Myself I abandon wholly to Thy will, O Lord. Just as I am Thy priest at the holy altar, I wish to be so all this day, wherever I shall be, with every soul who shall seek me in joy or in sorrow; let me remain, by Thy grace, I humbly beseech Thee, its mediator, unworthy though I be, for every excellent gift that descends from Thine abundance, through Jesus Christ Our Lord. Amen.

---

4 Hymn formerly used at Vespers for the Feast of the Most Holy Trinity: *O Lux beata Trinitas et principalis Unitas.*

LXXIII
ET VERBUM CARO FACTUM EST
AND THE WORD WAS MADE FLESH

Every day of the year, or almost every day, Thy Church, Lord Jesus, leads me again to this page, perhaps the most sacred of Thy holy Scripture. She would have me search it with the recollected gaze of my soul coming to it refreshed with Thy Holy Eucharist, with Thee; she would have this soul see itself therein in order, as it were, to conceive there every morning a new, a burning desire to resemble Thy Sanctity.

In principio erat Verbum. In the beginning, before all time, the Word was; He was with the Father, and this Word was God. This is the Ocean of divine Life into which Thou plungest me, O Jesus Christ, to conclude the series of innumerable graces Thou hast but now accorded me at the holy altar, me and all those surrounding me.

I plunge my being into Thee, O Word of the Father Who art Life eternal, without beginning or end, *Alpha and Omega, the beginning and the end of all things,* O God *Who art, and Who wast, and Who art to come, the Almighty,*[1] O Jesus Christ Who wast yesterday, Who art today, Who wilt be in all eternity. *Jesus Christus heri, et hodie, ipse et in saecula.*[2] Swallow me up in this Life in order that, dead to the other, to the life which is of man, I may live from that which is of God, which is God. *In ipso Vita erat.*[3]

Divine Wisdom, Art of the Father, Thou hast created all things, even to the invisible atom which acknowledges Him and adores Thee. *Thou Who didst create me, have mercy on me!* By every title I am Thine: as a creature who is the work of Thy Hands, as a Christian, and, above all, as Thy consecrated priest. Ah, yes, who is more completely Thine than a priest, the object of Thine unspeakable tenderness, and followed unweariedly by the gaze of Thy foreseeing Love!

---

1 Apoc. 1: 8.   2 Heb. 13: 8.   3 In Him was Life.

O Word, Light of Light, true God of true God, enlighten Thy priest, make Him Thy bearer of Christ; may souls see him as the candle *shining to all that are in Thy house*[4] or that may be so; even though they *sit in darkness and in the shadow of death.*[5] Be Thyself of this candle, the living flame that gives light to all men!

Yes, that is my vocation as priest: *I came*, like John the Baptist, Thy Precursor, *to give testimony of the Light which Thou art*. Apart from in this service as a witness, what am I, O Jesus Christ, and what could I be? I should but spoil my life and betray Thy call.

O Lord Jesus, on that day when, clothed in my chasuble, the symbol of love, I shall be, stretched out on my funeral couch, may it be said of me that I truly *received Thee,* God of the Eucharist, that I had faith in Thee, *the faithful and true,*[6] and that I was *born of God.*

Et Verbum Caro factum est.[7] O Jesus Christ, only support and supreme consolation of Thy priests, may it be said that I bore Thy divine stamp and that, in order to accomplish all Justice and realize Thy dream, I lived this definition of the Incarnation; yes, but in an inverted sense. May it be sung unto the glory of the Holy Trinity, unto the honor of the Church, unto the salvation of souls that *flesh was made the Word;* that this wretched flesh, this unclean slime, purified in Thy Blood, *me immundum munda tuo Sanguine,*[8] passed finally into the way of life of the Incarnate Word, was transformed into the radiant beauty of His Being, and that in all truth, it was not I who lived, but Jesus Christ in me.[9] *Et caro facta est Verbum.*

---

4 Matt. 5: 15.   5 Luke 1: 79.   6 Apoc. 19: 11.
7 And the Word was made Flesh.
8 Cleanse me, unclean, in Thy Blood (St Thomas).   9 Gal. 2: 20.

LXXIV
DEO GRATIAS
THANKS BE TO GOD

Deo Gratias! This is the last word of the Holy Mass and a complete definition of it, for *Eucharist* means *thanksgiving*. We have accomplished this Eucharist today; that is, through Jesus Christ, with Jesus Christ, and in Jesus Christ, we have sent up to the Holy Trinity the living and most holy canticle that sings Its supreme honor and glory, *omnis honor et gloria*.

Deo gratias! My God, I thank Thee, *Confiteor tibi, Pater.*[1] Thou hast heaped up the measure of Thy mercies for me today. Even supposing I could have celebrated the Holy Sacrifice but once in all my life, could have celebrated but the one Mass of my priestly ordination, the twenty-five years of preparation for it would still not have been too much, nor the twenty-five others that have since passed by. *Deo gratias!* My God, how good Thou hast been to me, today and all these many years!

Deo gratias! I feel myself powerless to thank Thee, just as I am powerless, without Thee, O Jesus Christ, to do anything whatsoever.[2] But I offer Thee; once more in my Thanksgiving, I offer Thee to the Holy Trinity, with Thy glorious wounds, which sing, in the celestial abode, the greatness of Thy gift and make the lasting power of Thy priesthood speak before the Face of God, *ut appareat nunc vultui Dei pro nobis.*[3] Thou art Thyself my Thanksgiving, O eternal Priest, eternal Victim, eternal Altar of God! That is what consoles, reassures, encourages me.

Hostia perpetua! That is the name given Thee by the Singer of Thy Eucharist, that Angelic Doctor whose virtues obtained for him the privilege of celebrating Thee in the immortal masterpiece of this Mass, which Thy most unworthy servant, O Jesus, has ventured to expound as well as he could in these meditations. Thou remainest the *Hostia perpetua*, the perpet-

---

1 I confess to Thee, O Father (Matt. 11: 25).   2 John 15: 5.
3 That He may appear now in the presence of God for us (Heb. 9: 24).

ual Victim of the Blessed Trinity, even in the midst of Thy heavenly glory; that has been so since Calvary, it is now, and will be so world without end; and with St Thomas, with all who believe in the power and wisdom and supreme goodness of Thine abundant Redemption, I give Thee thanks therefor. *Deo Gratias!*

Deo Gratias! In the words, *Hostia perpetua,* my own act of Thanksgiving is announced: I must be a perpetual Victim with Thee, Lord Jesus. I must be ever on the altar with Thee, at all hours, of the day and the night; for not a moment passes on this earth that does not see Thy Blood, which streams in torrents from the wound in Thy sacred side, gathered into the Chalice of Thy priests and offered to the honor and glory of the adorable Trinity.

Deo Gratias! My priestly life, the perfection of the simple Christian life and the supreme flowering, on this earth, of Baptismal grace, must be just that, and nothing but that: the immolation of a victim who lives by his oblation and unites it with Thine own, O Jesus Christ, Priest of priests, Victim of victims!

Quotidie morior.[4] I die daily; yes, Lord, put with Thee, my arms outstretched on Thy holy Cross, my hands in Thy hands, my feet in Thy feet, my side in Thy sacred side, my face pressed to Thine, O Most Holy Jesus; so will the same Precious Blood ever flow over me, so shall I be nailed with the same nails; so shall I constantly raise my voice with Thine in utterance of those Seven Words of Thine Agony on Calvary, that sublime hymn to our Heavenly Father which on the altar as well as on the Cross, measures the beat of each of the solemn moments in which Thy Redemption is accomplished for the salvation of the world.

Deo Gratias! O Father, into Thy hands I commend my spirit, through Jesus Christ my Lord! *Deo Gratias!*

---

4 1 Cor. 15: 31.

EPILOGUE

AVE, MARIA, GRATIA PLENA

HAIL, MARY, FULL OF GRACE

If thou, O Mary, art Mediatrix of all graces, then it was surely thou—I have never had any doubt of it—who didst obtain for me the grace of being consecrated as priest of thy Beloved Son, Our Lord Jesus Christ. For this, as for all else, be thou blessed, O Mary, blessed among women!

I can not bring to a close this work in which thou hast guided my hand without greeting thee and singing again to thy praise: *Ave Maria, gratia plena. Hail Mary, full of grace; the Lord is with thee: blessed art thou among women!* Ah, no, it is true thou didst never receive the consecration which we priests of Jesus have received and which makes us the ministers of the Most High. But I have read that, since no spiritual beauty could be lacking to thee, the hand of God having given thee every manner of adornment and embellished thee with the most varied forms of grace, it is inconceivable that so perfect a creature as thou could be deprived of the interior gifts reserved for priests, of the particular favors that are the endowment of the ministers of the sanctuary, or, finally, of the infused virtues which perfect priestly souls.[1]

Therefore, O Mary, I understand why the Fathers of the Church vie with each other in saluting thee with such titles as *priestly Virgin*,[2] *Queen of the ecclesiastical hierarchy and glory of the priesthood*,[3] *minister of Christ*,[4] *minister of holy joys*,[5] *chosen minister of the eternal Mystery*,[6] *splendid ornament of the celestial hierarchy, the joy and the glory of priests*,[7] and, finally, as

1 Mgr van den Berghe: *Mariae et le sacerdoce.*
2 St John of Damascus: Serm. 2 *in Nat. BMV.*
3 St Albertus Magnus: *super Missus est.*
4 St Augustine: *De Assumpt. BMV.*
5 St Andrew of Crete: *Orat. de Annunt.*
6 George of Nicomedia: *Orat. in Deip. ingress. in Templ.*
7 St Ephraim: *Orat. Laudes VM.*

the *offerer of prayers*,[8] placed by God between Jesus Christ and ourselves.

Ave Maria. I know one thing: the more I contemplate thy life, O Mary, the more I see it to have been an honorable sacrifice in which thou, also, didst enter into the functions of a priest and victim of Jesus, making thyself to this very day the model and teacher of priests and faithful, for lives which must be made as it were a living Mass.

Thou didst begin thy Mass when, presented in the Temple in thy tender childhood, and binding thyself there in vows of holy virginity, thou didst learn with most astounding humility the practice of holy compunction—of which for thee, the Immaculate, there was certainly no need—in order to weep for sins thou hadst never committed; but thy contrition accumulated a store of graces for us who should one day ask of thee the secret of holy tears.

There, in the Temple, thou didst penetrate as no other the mystery of the Sacred Scripture. Even long before the Angel Gabriel came to thee to make the blessed annunciation to thee of Jesus Christ, these Writings had, by an incomparably intense illumination of faith, revealed to thee this Word of the Father, the Word Who thus was born in thee spiritually before He became flesh in thy womb.

Thou didst make thine *Offertory*, O Mary, when, through love for God and man, thou wast able to reply to the Archangel sent by the Holy Trinity to receive thy freely given Fiat: *"Ecce Ancilla Domini*, behold the handmaid of *the Lord; be it done to me according to Thy Word."*[9] Within thy chaste being the Spirit of love then conceived this Word, Whose flesh thou preparedst with the most pure blood of thy blessed heart, with the blood which was one day to become the Precious Blood of Calvary and of the altar.

For thou hadst also thy *Consecration*, when, standing before the Cross thou madest offering in priestly attitude of this Blood which cleansed the world and when, a heroic Mother, renouncing Jesus as it were, thou, Co-redemptrice of souls, didst accept, didst receive in adoption, the Son of Zebedee for the Son of God, John for Jesus, and not the one alone, but all men, even those who are crucifying Him and thereby plunging into thy heart the sword foretold by holy Simeon.

Thou hadst thine intimate *Communion* when, clasping thy Beloved Son in thy arms and tenderly sorrowing over all His wounds, one by one, thy

---

8 St John of Damascus: *in Octoed. Graec.* 9 Luke 1: 38.

compassion made these wounds thine and likened thee to the *perpetual Victim* of time and of eternity.

O Mary, Virgin Mother of priests, today and every day of my life I will keep near thee; there, where St John stood, the disciple whom Jesus loved, the priest singled out by His love, there will I stand; I will stay by the Cross with thee, gazing upon Him, this Jesus crucified, Whom alone it is necessary for a priest to know, to love, and to preach. *Scire Jesum et hunc crucifixum.*[10] *Nos autem praedicamus Christum crucifixum ... scandalum ... stultitiam.*[11] Men will not always understand: some will cry scandal, others foolishness. What is that to me? For it has pleased God that the priest, by preaching this foolishness, should save them that believe. *Per stultitiam praedicationis.*[12]

O Mary, teach the priest of Jesus *this folly of the Cross, the true Wisdom in the eyes of God and the solemn manifestation of His power.*[13] Teach in how I may be transformed into Jesus crucified; how, like the Apostle, I may come to bear in my body the marks of the Lord Jesus. *Ego enim stigmata Domini Jesu in corpore meo porto.*[14]

Thine answer, O Mother, is that I shall learn that at the holy altar, *the mountain of myrrh and the hill of frankincense,*[15] the blessed ascension of which I shall make each morning with thee in order to enter into the wounds of Jesus crucified.

Ah, may I come down therefrom every day a little more nearly *likened to the Son of God,*[16] ever more truly conscious of my awe-inspiring vocation, and determined to be nothing less than a saint in it, that I may give all honor and glory to the sanctity of the sublime High Priest, the Lord Jesus Christ, to Whom be adoration and love forever and ever. Amen.

---

10 To know Jesus Christ and Him crucified (1 Cor. 2: 2).
11 But we preach Christ crucified ... a stumbling block ... foolishness (*Ibid.* 1: 23).
12 By the foolishness of our preaching (*Ibid.* 1: 21).   13 *Ibid.* 1: 17–25.
14 For I bear the marks of the Lord Jesus in my body (Gal. 6: 17).
15 Cant. 4: 6.   16 Heb. 7: 3.

About The Cenacle Press at Silverstream Priory

An apostolate of the Benedictine monastery of Silverstream Priory in Ireland, the mission of The Cenacle Press can be summed up in four words: *Quis ostendit nobis bona*—who will show us good things (Psalm 4:6)? In an age of confusion, ugliness, and sin, our aim is to show something of the Highest Good to every reader who picks up our books. More specifically, we believe that the treasury of the centuries-old Benedictine tradition and the beauty of holiness which has characterized so many of its followers through the ages has something beneficial, worthwhile, and encouraging in it for every believer.

cenaclepress.com

Also Available:

Robert Hugh Benson
The Friendship of Christ

Robert Hugh Benson
Confessions of a Convert

Fr Willie Doyle, SJ
Pamphlets for the Faithful

Dom Pius de Hemptinne, OSB
A Benedictine Soul: Biography, Letters, and Spiritual Writings of Dom Pius de Hemptinne

Blessed Columba Marmion, OSB
Christ the Ideal of the Monk

Blessed Columba Marmion, OSB
Words of Life on the Margin of the Missal

St John Henry Newman (*ed.* Melinda Nielsen)
Festivals of Faith: Sermons for the Liturgical Year

Fr Ryan T. Sliwa
New Nazareths in Us

Dom Hubert van Zeller, OSB
Approach to Prayer

Dom Hubert van Zeller, OSB
Sanctity in Other Words

Visit www.cenaclepress.com for our full catalogue.